BOOKS BY ROBERT JAY LIFTON

Home from the War
Explorations in Psychohistory (*editor, with Eric Olson*)
Living and Dying (*with Eric Olson*)
History and Human Survival
Boundaries: Psychological Man in Revolution
Death in Life: Survivors of Hiroshima
Revolutionary Immortality: Mao Tse-tung and the Chinese
    Cultural Revolution
Thought Reform and the Psychology of Totalism
Birds
Crimes of War (*editor, with Richard Falk and*
    Gabriel Kolko)
America and the Asian Revolutions (*editor*)
The Woman in America (*editor*)
The Life of the Self: Toward a New Psychology

The Life of the Self

TOWARD A NEW PSYCHOLOGY

Robert Jay Lifton

Simon and Schuster : New York

Copyright © 1976 by Robert Jay Lifton
All rights reserved
including the right of reproduction
in whole or in part in any form
Published by Simon and Schuster
A Gulf+Western Company
Rockefeller Center, 630 Fifth Avenue
New York, New York 10020

Designed by Irving Perkins
Manufactured in the United States of America

1 2 3 4 5 6 7 8 9 10

Library of Congress Cataloging in Publication Data

Lifton, Robert Jay
    The life of the self.

    Includes bibliographical references and index.
    1. Psychology.   2. Symbolism (Psychology)
3. Psychoanalysis.   I. Title.   [DNLM: 1. Death.
2. Ego.   3. Psychology.   BF38 L722L]
BF38.L55   150'.19'5   75-41470
ISBN 0-671-22219-8

We are grateful for permission to reprint:

Excerpt from *Cat's Cradle* by Kurt Vonnegut, Jr., copyright © 1963 by
Kurt Vonnegut, Jr. Reprinted by permission of Delacorte Press/Seymour
Lawrence.

From "The Sense of Immortality: On Death and the Continuity of
Life," reprinted by permission of the Editor of *The American Journal
of Psychoanalysis*, 1973, Vol. 33, No. 1, pp. 3–15.

"The Struggle for Cultural Rebirth" originally appeared in *Harper's
Magazine*, April 1973, Vol. 246. •

From "The Survivor as Creator," reprinted from *The American Poetry
Review*, Vol. 2, No. 1.

ACKNOWLEDGMENTS

Conversations with colleagues at Yale and with psychiatric residents during seminars I gave on some of these subjects have taught me much. So have dialogues at the Wellfleet summer meetings on psychohistory over the past ten years—especially with Kenneth Keniston, Norman Birnbaum, Margaret Brenman-Gibson, Peter Brooks, Robert Holt and Richard Sennet. My homage to Erik H. Erikson is, I hope, apparent both in my acknowledgment of his work and in my "deviations" from it. Eric Olson has discussed many of the book's ideas with me, and also did valuable editing of the manuscript. Alice Mayhew, my editor at Simon and Schuster, helped on many levels to bring the book into being. Lily Finn devotedly typed and coordinated its many drafts. Betty Jean Lifton has been with me through everything, including discussions of the work.

I wish also to acknowledge help received in this work, over years, from the Foundations Fund for Research in Psychiatry, the Hazen Foundation, the Harry Frank Guggenheim Foundation, and the Rockefeller Foundation.

Portions of this volume have appeared, in very different form, in the following publications: *Journal of the American Academy of Psychoanalysis, American Journal of Psychoanalysis, Salmagundi, Harper's,* the *American Poetry Review, Omega,* the *History of Childhood Quarterly,* and the *International Journal of Psychoanalysis.*

For Eric Olson

—FELLOW EXPLORER OF FORMS

Contents

What we need for a science of mind is not so much a definitive concept of mind, as a conceptual frame in which to lodge our observations of mental phenomena.
—Susanne K. Langer

I am dreaming and I would
act well, for good deeds
are not lost, even in dreams.
—Pedro Calderón

Introduction

In much of my work I have expressed ideas that, from the standpoint of prevailing views in psychoanalysis, could be said to be heretical. But there comes a moment when we can no longer speak of heresy, when both dogma and opposition to it are dwarfed by the larger demands of a major historical turning point. At such a moment it is no less arrogant to insist upon one's particular heresy than upon the eternal truth of one's particular dogma. One does better to build and connect, to weave the threads of heresy into a pattern that reaches back to the spirit behind the dogma and forward to the consciousness struggling to take shape.

This book is an attempt to provide the contours of an evolving point of view or conceptual frame—an evolving paradigm—in psychological work, with emphasis upon its sources as well as its reach. I try to articulate and order principles I have been developing over a number of studies and writings, and to locate these principles in past and contemporary thought. By rendering these psychological concepts in their most basic and systematic form I seek to make them more accessible to myself. If I succeed in that, I know they will be more accessible to others.

On several occasions, when I was presenting some of the ideas put forward in this book to professional audiences, people responded by saying something like "You have put into words and organized a lot of ideas and feelings many of us

13

have had in our work for some time." I was of course very pleased by such comments, but as I thought about them I realized that they signified something quite beyond my own efforts. For although my focus is on the sequence from Freud to Erikson to my own and others' work, the new paradigm has still broader roots that have affected large numbers of investigators and practitioners.

In the work of such gifted predecessors as Rank, Adler, Jung, Fromm, Rado, and Horney, one encounters elements of the formative principle I advocate—of stress on a symbolizing process involving continuous creation and transformation of psychic structures (images and forms) on behalf of the many-sided life (and in response to the threatened or anticipated death) of the self. In particular, the three great early "defectors," Adler, Jung, and Rank, could be said to have broken with Freud (apart from their personal conflicts with him) around issues of symbolization. On the issue of "incest taboo," for instance, all three stressed suprapersonal, nonsexual (that is, symbolic) elements having to do with family continuity and community, in opposition to Freud's focus on the more literal expression of the taboo in individual psychology, in the "Oedipus complex." Hence Jung, in his posthumous autobiography, claimed that while working on his early study of transformations of the libido, "I knew in advance that its publication would cost me my friendship with Freud [because] to me incest signified a personal complication only in the rarest case. . . . But Freud clung to the literal interpretation of it and could not grasp the spiritual significance of incest as a symbol." Rank, in turn, came to view the entire Oedipus myth as a creation rite, involving the killing of the "old Year-god" by the "new Year-god" or "Year-king." Rank also associated the myth with the emergence of relatively stable Greek family life—with the father rebelling against the role of the father and the son against the role of the son—as well as with related myths of twinship (which Rank relates to his concept of "the double") in which the hero must kill his twin brother in order to assert his immortal self.

In related ways Fromm and Horney have stressed the creative possibilities in the mind's capacity for symbolization. Fromm associated that capacity with the "forgotten language" of the unconscious, which renders us in our dreams "not only less reasonable and less decent . . . but . . . also more intelligent, wiser, and capable of better judgment . . . than when we are awake." This view contrasts sharply with Freud's relatively literal emphasis upon the infantile psychosexual origins of dreams, and upon their motivational source in "the wish." Yet it took the work of Cassirer and Langer to demonstrate the truly radical potential of the concept of symbolization—its possibilities for raising questions at the heart of human knowledge and motivation.

Consider, for instance, the matter of the dream image. When it is viewed as part of constantly active symbolizations, one can no longer speak of "recovering" or "remembering" such an image, at least in its original form. For that image, like all expressions of the psyche, is subject to the historical principle of Heraclitus: "You cannot step twice into the same river, for other waters are constantly flowing in." Those "waters" include all currents that influence the mind seeking to remember the dream. In that sense one can never precisely "interpret" a dream or any other constellation of images; one can merely get in touch with their flow. That formative principle, of "getting in touch with the flow" of structure and meaning, can be utilized not only in direct psychological observation but in examining the contesting claims—symbolic forms—of competing schools of psychological thought. It is the means by which one can move beyond Freudian and neo-Freudian entrenchments and evolve desperately needed new concepts, even as one reconnects with the vitality of the master.

All this takes time. I have often wondered why classical psychoanalytic theory has generally prevailed (especially in the United States, but elsewhere as well) against "deviationist" or "revisionist" writers and schools, even when the revisions seemed to improve the theory and put it more in touch with recent thought. Part of the explanation lies in the comprehensiveness and systematic structure of Freud's opus, which has enabled it to provide consistent, readily transmissible ideas for generations of students and practitioners, in contrast to the more sporadic insights and hand-to-mouth intellectual fare of revisionist theories. But I would suggest a somewhat different, though related, explanation. Freud's revolutionary breakthrough lay in no single psychological discovery so much as in the creation of a totally new psychological paradigm—a new set of assumptions about human nature and function, and about ways of studying the human psyche and of healing its patterns of dysfunction. To be sure there were significant weaknesses in that paradigm almost from its beginning, as followers-turned-deviationists rightly perceived. But so revolutionary a paradigm had to have time to work itself out—to be made use of, tried out in theory and therapy, appreciated and criticized in action—before anything like a community of psychological thinkers could begin to embrace an altered version of it or an alternative.

Are we now ready to take that step? It is difficult to say. In the world of psychoanalytical psychiatry it is sometimes hard to tell whether "change is in the air" or merely that it should be. The truth is that so many divergent critiques and currents contend for our recognition that one cannot easily find in them a consistent pattern. But there are a number of contemporary currents related to this study, currents that have been around for some time but are now ready to make greater claim on us.

First, there is the idea of fundamental shift—or paradigm change—in psychological thought, suggested various times in the past, and recently in a provocative way by Edgar Levenson in *The Fallacy of Understanding*. Second, the organizing principle of death and continuity, which I found first in Rank, and has been given brilliant recent expression by Ernest Becker in his *The Denial of Death*. Third, the principle of formation and symbolization in psychological work—suggested in different ways by Gestalt psychology and the writings of Kurt Goldstein, Silvano Arieti, and Marshall Edelson. (Here the original influences for me were the philosophical writings of Ernst Cassirer, Susanne Langer, and L. L. Whyte, though there are also close parallels with various strands of what we now call "structuralism.") Fourth, the emphasis upon thinking and knowing sometimes described under the rubric of "cognitive psychology" as developed by Jean Piaget and Jerome Bruner, and of "ego psychology" by Robert Holt and George Klein. Fifth, the historical or "psychohistorical" dimension, long a concern in the work of a number of us—including Kenneth Keniston and Robert Coles —following upon the breakthrough achieved by Erik Erikson. (This psychohistorical approach, when combined with a formative-symbolic one, approaches a wholistic sense of interacting elements of a kind now stressed in "systems theory.") Finally, there is what might be called the psychology of experience and transcendence—as epitomized by the writings of Ronald D. Laing and Norman O. Brown—toward which the paradigm I suggest can, I believe, provide a necessary combination of receptivity and critical perspective.

In connecting with each of these seemingly unrelated currents, I seek the beginnings of a theoretical structure that is sufficiently integrated to provide a base to build from, and sufficiently open-ended for that further construction to occur. To date many suggested revisions of Freudian theory, in their very wisdom, have been at odds with still unquestioned assumptions within the overall Freudian paradigm. The result is often a confusing array of truth and contradiction—of islands of insight awaiting the integrative structure within which they might find a lasting place. And the entire enterprise is impeded by lingering nineteenth-century assumptions about science, about this particular cause resulting in that particular effect and either-or approaches to truth—assumptions which, though long abandoned by other sciences, still prevent psychological investigators from "getting in touch with the flow." The structure I put forward, then, is inclusive and wide-ranging, more than an outline but far less than an exhaustive study.

The paradigm shift is influenced by various currents in our contemporary history. It is also, I would add, related to trends in the human evolutionary process. For, as I will suggest, our strange new closeness to sources of life on the one hand and to species extinction on the other renders cultural evolution and history considerably less distinct from each other in their time dimensions. If a new historical consciousness is emerging, as I believe it is, we must also speak of a significant shift, if not mutation, in cultural evolution. We would expect an emerging psychological paradigm to connect with (or at least be open to) a new evolutionary awareness. A case in point is the developing discipline of "sociobiology," which lays great stress on what Edward O. Wilson calls the "prime movers of evolution" in shaping the biological basis for social behavior. I believe that the approach described in this book can make useful contact with that discipline, as already suggested by certain parallel lines of thought and even common language. (See footnote on pages 62–63.)

A fundamental contemporary link between psychology and evolution is the human capacity for symbolization. That capacity in itself (as Cassirer wrote and Theodosius Dobzhansky quotes approvingly in relationship to evolutionary theory) "transforms the whole of human life [so that] man lives not merely in a broader reality—he lives, so to speak, in a new *dimension* of reality." The "new dimension" is, in turn, inseparable from another evolutionary principle contained in the new paradigm, that of death and continuity. Depth psychology has been too long recognizing the central evolutionary theme of life continuity and its significance for individual and generational struggles around mortality and connection. Perhaps it takes our present apocalyptic threats to the overall evolutionary process to jar our profession from its complacency. But how can we call ourselves psychologists if we ignore either that threat or the accompanying human hunger and potential for an evolutionary leap?

Within this evolutionary and historical context, death becomes a many-sided psychological issue—or what has been called a complex symbol. Death is first (and, no doubt, last) the end of life—an inevitable, routine aspect of the rhythms of beginnings, middles, and ends encompassed by what we call nature. In that sense death is crucial to the natural-selection process of evolution, as it is to the endings and new beginnings within human history. For the individual, death is a built-in (though I would not say "instinctual") organic *and psychological* destiny perceived through imagery of termination and nothingness.

A second meaning of death has to do with a psychological equivalent—the idea of "death in life," of loss of vitality of feeling, or what I speak of as psychic numbing. This is what

Kurt Vonnegut has in mind when he associates much of the trouble in the world with the fact that too many people in high places are "stone cold dead." Death becomes a model for life, life an imitation of death. Here death is a negative symbol for stasis, severed connection, disintegration.

A third aspect of death is perhaps the most neglected: death as a formative or constitutive symbol, an element of creativity and renewal. Death then symbolizes the human capacity to confront in some way the most fearful aspects of experience and emerge with deepened sensibility and extended vitality and reach. This is what Heinrich Böll had in mind when he said, "The artist carries death in him like a good priest his breviary." Maintaining a psychic place for death, that is, enhances that which is most human, the imagination.

A new sensitivity to the impact of death on the human imagination is crucial to any next step in depth psychology. But that sensitivity in itself is not enough. What is needed, I believe, is a fundamental (if not agonizing) reappraisal, one that addresses itself to the larger organizing principles that subsume our everyday working concepts—one that addresses itself to issues of paradigm and paradigm shift. Only in that way can those of us who grope our way along the byways of depth psychology claim a new relationship to science, to our profession, and to ourselves. Within that project I see this book as a passionate, schematic, and vulnerable beginning.

CHAPTER 1

The Paradigm in Psychological Science

I want to begin with a statement midway between an observation and a declaration: We are now in the relatively early phases of a momentous shift in psychological paradigm—a shift away from both the classical psychoanalytic model of instinct and defense, and even from the approach and perspective inherent in the word "analysis" itself.

The indications are everywhere around us: the deep uneasiness, bordering on despair, of large numbers of practitioners and investigators as they experience threats to the validity of the existing classical paradigm along with an absence of a new paradigm sufficiently powerful to replace it; the widely felt though often inchoate sense that we are losing rather than gaining ground in our struggles to cope professionally with the increasingly formidable social and psychological forces that confront us; and the atmosphere of chaotic eclecticism, within which it becomes difficult indeed to distinguish narrow dogma and intensified cultism from sustained commitment, superficiality from bold experiment, and excessive claim from genuine accomplishment.

In all this the psychological professions are hardly alone. Other disciplines, probably without exception, suffer similarly; they share with us the confusions and possibilities that accompany the vast contemporary breakdown of viable cultural symbolizations and forms that I have elsewhere spoken of as "psychohistorical dislocation." But there is special poignancy and pain in our particular situation of being both caught up in this dislocation and charged with the responsibility for describing and interpreting the ways in which people experience it.

My basic premise is that we understand man through paradigms or models. The choice of the paradigm or model becomes extremely important, because it determines what might be called the "controlling image" or central theme of our psychological theory. Human culture is sufficiently rich that a great variety of paradigms are available to serve as controlling images, including those of "power," "being," "instinct and defense," "social class," "collective unconscious," "interpersonal relations," etc. These paradigms are by no means of equal merit, but each can be used to illuminate some aspect of human experience.

I shall use the word "paradigm" in the sense derived from physical science, while suggesting important differences in its applicability to depth psychology. In Chapter 2 I suggest the contours of a formative depth psychology in which death and symbolization of life continuity are given a central place. In the succeeding two chapters I trace what I believe are shifts in paradigm from Freud to Erikson to the directions of my own work. My hope is that this exploration can further the shift, which I believe to be necessary; suggest a more specific and less defensive relationship to scientific tradition; and help to articulate what depth psychologists do in general and what I am trying to do in particular.

Responding to criticisms of his concept of paradigm, Thomas S. Kuhn admits using the word "in two different senses." "On the one hand," he tells us, "it stands for the entire constellation of beliefs, values, techniques, and so on shared by the members of a given [scientific] community," while "on the other, it denotes one sort of element in that constellation, the concrete puzzle-solutions which, employed as models or examples, can replace explicit rules [of earlier paradigms] as a basis for the solution of the remaining puzzles of normal science."[1] Whatever the confusion between the two meanings, Kuhn's work demonstrates how much they overlap and depend upon each other. For precisely that shared constellation of beliefs and images held within a scientific community provides the models or "exemplars" that enable an individual scientist "to see his problem as *like* a problem he has already encountered."

Paradigms, then, "define the legitimate problems and methods of a research field for succeeding generations of practitioners." They can do so only when they possess two crucial characteristics. Their scientific "achievement" must be "sufficiently unprecedented" to win over "an enduring group of adherents" from competing modes of scientific practice. And they must be "sufficiently open-ended" to leave many problems unresolved. For, as Kuhn explains, a paradigm is not so much "an object for replication" as for "further . . . specification under new or more stringent conditions." A new paradigm gains its status by demonstrating itself "more successful than . . . competitors in solving . . . problems that the group of practitioners has come to recognize as acute." That success is at first largely potential, and is realized only through continuing application in everyday "normal science," whose function consists of "the actualization of that promise . . . achieved by extending the knowledge of

those facts that the paradigm displays as particularly revealing, by increasing the extent of the match between those
facts and the paradigm's predictions, and by further articulation of the paradigm itself."

Those who fail to accept the new paradigm—who do not
recognize its greater relevance and precision or do not adopt
its "more stringent conditions" and "more rigid definition of
the field"—become increasingly isolated. For natural science
has rather clear-cut ways of measuring success, whatever its
contemporary awareness of relativism, indeterminancy, and
the influence of the observer. Hence those who fail to adopt
the more productive new paradigm "are simply read out
of the profession, which thereafter ignores their work," and
in that way "the older schools gradually disappear."

Applying this view of the paradigm to our experience in
depth psychology, I am impressed by the degree to which its
general principles hold. But there is one fundamental quali-
fication. Depth-psychological work is simply not, in its very
nature, comparably precise in concepts or observations, nor
comparably susceptible to proof or disproof. It is radically
less predictive and notoriously more complex in its many-
layered, unmanageable variables. Just this combination of
similarity and difference has created a false debate within
depth psychology. On one side are those who insist upon
exact adherence to the criteria and models of natural science
(the philosophical point of view of Freud and many of his
followers, whatever their imaginative habits). On the other
side are those who wish to achieve total separation of depth
psychology from natural science (many—but by no means all
—practitioners of "existential" or "humanistic" psychology).

But surely science at its noblest—as the ordering of knowledge—can encompass these distinctions between the physical
and psychological disciplines. And I am convinced that we

as depth psychologists can deepen our enterprise by continuing to relate it to the framework and tradition of science, while insisting upon a certain autonomy from physical science and a complete autonomy from positivistic definitions of *our* science.* The absence of this kind of appropriate and confident relationship to science contributes greatly, I believe, to those anxious expressions of ideological totalism that break out all too frequently among us—to the inappropriate embrace of the dogmatic poles of both science and religion in the attempt to "read" opponents "out of the profession" and thereby maintain the illusion that we possess precisely that which must elude our grasp: reliably predictive, provable, incontestible truth.

A central dilemma here for depth psychology is its extreme susceptibility to specific historical imagery and conflict. That imagery, moreover, directly reflects the prevailing sense among the people of a particular culture and epoch of their own nature. To be sure, physical science too is subject to historically specific imagery—as Gerald Holton has convincingly demonstrated[3]—but its relationship to such imagery is more general and indirect, less determinative of the outcome of its paradigms. Depth psychology, in contrast, must draw upon the individual and collective experience of its era in evolving its concept of the self; and then, in a subtle chain (or web) of cause and effect, turn that self on the self—apply it to the understanding of the individual. At that point the enterprise becomes unique to psychology.

At the end of my study of Hiroshima, *Death in Life*, I stated that sexuality and moralism had been the central themes confronted by Freud in developing psychoanalysis,

---

* Harry Guntrip similarly calls for "a nondeterministic, non-Positivistic, teleological theory . . . to aid us in the study of the psychodynamic phenomena of human beings as persons in relationships."[2]

but that now unlimited technological violence and absurd death have become more pressing themes for contemporary man.[4] During the Victorian era, when Freud was evolving his ideas, there was an overwhelming repression of sexuality but a relatively greater openness to the reality of human death. There has been a historical shift, and the contemporary situation is one in which we are less overwhelmed by sexual difficulties but more overwhelmed by difficulties around death.

The fact that Freud's model of libido and repression of instinctual sexual impulses was put forth during the late Victorian era, at a time when society was struggling with these issues, does not invalidate the generalizability of his ideas; their power lies precisely in that generalizability. But it does raise the important point—not only for Freud but for our own work now—of the influence of historical forces on the psychological theories we choose to develop. If we now begin to build psychological theory around death, it is because death imposes itself upon us in such unmanageable ways.

In my own psychological work on extreme historical situations involving ultimate violence and massive death, I have preferred to speak of a process of psychic numbing rather than repression. Repression occurs when an idea or experience is forgotten, excluded from consciousness, or relegated to the realm of the unconscious. Repressed childhood memories and repressed instinctual impulses are illustrations of this process. Repression is part of a model or controlling image characterized by drives and defenses and refers to the compensatory effort of the organism to cope with innate or instinctual forces that dominate emotional life. The original idea was to analyze these forces and thereby bring the patient to cure.

Psychoanalysis has been changed significantly by the development of ego psychology, by various neo-Freudian modifications, and by many new influences, including ethology. But I think that psychoanalytic theory is still bedeviled by its traditional imagery of instinct, repression, and defense. This imagery yields limited and distorted insight when one approaches the subject of death and the relationship of death to larger contemporary experience. The concept of psychic numbing, in contrast, suggests the cessation of what I call the formative process, the impairment of man's essential mental function of symbol formation or symbolization. This point of view is strongly influenced by the symbolic philosophy of Cassirer and Langer.[5] Psychic numbing is a form of desensitization; it refers to an incapacity to feel or to confront certain kinds of experience, due to the blocking or absence of inner forms or imagery that can connect with such experience.

The importance of this kind of phenomenon was impressed upon me very profoundly by my work in Hiroshima. And there can be little doubt that the technology of destruction has had a strong impact on the spread of psychic numbing. But my assumption is that psychic numbing is central in everyday experience as well, and may be identified whenever there is interference in the "formative" mental function, the process of creating viable inner forms. Central to the "psychoformative" perspective is the principle that a human being can never simply *receive* a bit of information nakedly. The process of perception is vitally bound up with the process of inner re-creation, in which one utilizes whatever forms are available in individual psychic existence.

I want to emphasize at the beginning that this approach to psychology and history is impelled by a sense of urgency about our present historical predicament, and by a strong desire to evolve psychohistorical theory adequate to the dangerous times in which we live. In this approach it is necessary to make our own subjectivity as investigators clear and conscious, to try to understand it and use it as part of our conceptual structure. In the final chapter I will suggest further implications of this harnessed subjectivity and some relationships of our own advocacies to the historical process.

I am not suggesting that there is no psychological baseline beyond historically specific imagery. Rather, the awareness of one's special sensitivity to that imagery enables one to achieve a more delicate and ultimately more humane understanding of oneself as a psychologist and "the other." With that awareness, the "scientific problem" of historical susceptibility can be seen simultaneously as an opening toward the special kinds of insight we are best equipped to pursue. And from such a perspective on the various disciplines, we can envision a continuum that extends from, at the one end, paradigms that are only approximate and highly dependent upon historical imagery to, at the other, those that are *relatively* more precise, predictive, and independent of historical constraint—from art and literature to history to social science to psychology to biology to physics to mathematics. Depth-psychological paradigms, more or less in the middle position of this continuum, have special characteristics that we must examine if we are to delineate the shift I am suggesting.

CHAPTER 2

On Death and Continuity

Serious concern with the way in which people confront death leads one to question the nature of death and the nature of life in the face of death. In my work in Hiroshima I found that studying an extreme situation such as that facing the survivors of the atomic bomb can lead to insights about everyday death, about ordinary people facing what Kurt Vonnegut has called "plain old death." Our psychological ideas about death have become so stereotyped, so limited and impoverished, that exposure to a holocaust like Hiroshima, or My Lai, or the entire American involvement in Indochina, forces us to develop new ideas and hypotheses that begin to account for some of the reactions that we observe. I want to suggest a few such principles that are both psychological and historical.

Fundamental to the formative paradigm in depth psychology is an emphasis on *death and the continuity of life*. In elaborating this aspect of the paradigm I will consider first the theory of symbolic immortality, then a related theory of evolving death imagery, and finally the application of this paradigm in clinical work and psychopathology.

Death and the continuity of life is actually man's oldest and most fundamental image for understanding human existence. But it has been remarkably ignored in psychological thought. Psychiatrists and psychoanalysts have for the most part left the question of death to philosophers. Freud's theory legitimized this neglect when he said:

> It is indeed impossible to imagine our own death: and whenever we attempt to do so we can perceive that we are in fact still present as spectators. Hence the psychoanalytic school could venture on the assertion that at bottom no one believes in his own death, or, to put the same thing in another way, that in his unconscious, every one of us is convinced of his own immortality.[1]

Freud viewed all interest in immortality as compensatory, as a denial of death and a refusal to face it unflinchingly. Freud insisted that we look at death squarely. He argued that psychologically we cannot afford the consequences of denial. But Freud had no place in his system for the *symbolic* significance of the idea of immortality as an expression of continuity. For this reason I call Freud's approach "rationalist-iconoclastic."

Jung's approach was very different; he took the mythological and symbolic aspects of death and immortality very seriously. His study of mythology convinced him of the enormous importance of the idea of immortality for the conscious and unconscious aspects of the human psyche. But he also said: "As a physician I am convinced that it is hygienic to discover in death a goal toward which one can strive, and that shrinking away from it is something unhealthy and abnormal"; and "I . . . consider the religious teaching of a life hereafter consonant with the standpoint of psychic hygiene."[2] In such statements it becomes unclear whether Jung is talking about the literal idea of a life after death or a more symbolic one. He surrenders much of the scientific viewpoint, however broadly defined, that man has struggled for so painfully over the last few centuries. We can thus call Jung's approach "hygienic-mythical."

Both of these views are important; neither is completely satisfactory. Freud's attitude has the merit of unflinching acceptance of death as a total annihilation of the organism. Jung's view has the merit of stressing the symbolic significance of universal imagery around death and immortality.

A third perspective—which I shall call "formative-symbolic" —draws upon both Freud and Jung but takes into account the increasing awareness of symbol formation as a fundamental characteristic of man's psychic life. I should emphasize that I am speaking of an ongoing *process of symbolization,* rather than of particular symbols (the flag, the cross, etc.). In classical psychoanalysis the focus tends to be on symbols as specific equivalents—pencil for penis, sea for mother, etc.—and much less upon the more fundamental process of creation and re-creation of images and forms that characterizes human mentation.

I would hold, in the context of this psychoformative view, that even in our unconscious lives we are by no means *convinced* of our own immortality. Rather, we have what some recent workers have called "middle knowledge"[3] of the idea of death. We both "know" that we will die and resist and fail to act upon that knowledge. Nor is the need to transcend death *mere* denial. More essentially, it represents a compelling universal urge to maintain an inner sense of continuous symbolic relationship, over time and space, with the various elements of life. In other words, I am speaking of a *sense* of immortality as in itself neither compensatory nor pathological, but as man's symbolization of his ties with both his biological fellows and his history, past and future. This view is consistent with Otto Rank's stress on man's perpetual

need for "an assurance of eternal survival for his self." Rank
suggested that "man creates culture by changing natural conditions in order to maintain his spiritual self."⁴ But this need
for a sense of symbolic immortality, interwoven with man's
biology and his history, is for the most part ignored by in-
dividually biased psychological theory.

The sense of immortality can be expressed in five general
modes. The first and most obvious is the biological mode, the
sense of living on *through* and *in* one's sons and daughters
and their sons and daughters. At some level of consciousness
we imagine an endless chain of biological attachments. This
mode has been a classical expression of symbolic immortality
in East Asian culture, especially in traditional China, with its
extraordinary emphasis on the family line. In Confucian eth-
ics, the greatest of all unfilial acts is lack of posterity. But this
mode never remains purely biological; it becomes simultaneously biosocial, and expresses itself in attachments to one's
group, tribe, organization, people, nation or even species.
Ultimately one can feel at least glimmerings of a sense of immortality in "living on" through and in mankind.

A second expression of the sense of immortality is the theological idea of a life after death or, more importantly, the idea
of release from profane life to existence on a higher plane.
The literal idea of an afterlife is not essential to this mode,
and such a notion is not present in many religions. More basic
is the concept of transcending death through spiritual attainment. The power of spiritual life to overcome death in some
way is exemplified in all the great religious leaders around
whom religions have been founded: Buddha, Moses, Christ,
Mohammed. Within each of the religious traditions there has
been a word to convey the spiritual state in which one has
transcended death: the Japanese word *kami*, the Polynesian
term *mana*, the Roman idea of noumen, the Eskimo concept

of tungnik, and the Christian doctrine of grace. All these words describe a state in which one possesses spiritual power over death, meaning, in a symbolic sense, that one is in harmony with a principle extending beyond the limited biological life span.

The third mode of symbolic immortality is that achieved through "works": the mode of creativity, the achievement of enduring human impact, the sense that one's writing, one's teaching, one's human influences, great or humble, will live on, that one's contribution will not die. The therapeutic efforts of physicians and psychotherapists are strongly impelled, I believe, by an image of therapeutic impact extending through the patient to others, including the patient's children, in an endless potentially beneficent chain of influence. The "therapeutic despair" described so sensitively by Leslie Farber[5] as an occupational hazard of the psychiatrist treating schizophrenic patients might well result from the perception that one's strenuous therapeutic endeavors are not producing these lasting effects, that one's energies are not animating the life of the patient and cannot therefore symbolically extend one's own.

A fourth mode is the sense of immortality through being survived by nature itself: the theme of eternal nature. This theme is very vivid among the Japanese, and was one of the most important kinds of imagery for survivors of the atomic bomb. It is strong not only in Shinto belief, but in the European Romantic movement and in the Anglo-Saxon cult of the great outdoors—indeed, in every culture in one form or another.

The fifth mode is somewhat different from the others in that it depends solely upon a psychic state. This is the state of "experiential transcendence," a state so intense that in it time and death disappear. When one achieves ecstasy or rapture, the restrictions of the senses—including the sense of mortality—no longer exist. Poetically and religiously this has been described as "losing oneself." It can occur not only in religious or secular mysticism but also in song, dance, battle, sexual love, childbirth, athletic effort, mechanical flight, or in contemplating works of artistic or intellectual creation.[6] This state is characterized by extraordinary psychic unity and perceptual intensity. But there also occurs, as we hear described in drug experiences, a process of symbolic reordering. One feels oneself to be different after returning from this state. I see experiential transcendence and its aftermath as epitomizing the death-and-rebirth experience. It is central to change or transformation and has great significance for psychotherapy. Experiential transcendence includes a feeling of what Eliade has called "continuous present" that can be equated with eternity or with "mythical time."[7] This continuous present is perceived not only as "here and now" but as inseparable from past and future.

The theory of symbolic immortality can be used to illuminate changes in cultural emphasis from one historical period to another. We can think of historical shifts as involving alterations in the stress given to one or another mode or combinations of modes. The Darwinian revolution of the nineteenth century, for example, can be seen as entailing a shift from a predominantly theological mode to a more natural and biological one. The continuous transformation in China over the last few decades involves a shift from a family-centered biological mode to a revolutionary mode. I have elsewhere described this revolutionary mode as emphasizing human works but as including also elements of other modes with periodic emphasis upon experiential transcendence.[8]

Following the holocausts of World War II the viability of psychic activity within the modes has undergone something of a collapse, at least in the West. We exist now in a time of doubt about modes of continuity and connection, and I believe this has direct relevance for work with individual patients. Awareness of our historical predicament—of threats posed by nuclear weapons, environmental destruction, and the press of rising population against limited resources—has created extensive imagery of extinction. These threats occur at a time when the rate of historical velocity with its resulting psychohistorical dislocation has already undermined established symbols around the institutions of family, church, government, and education.

Combined imagery of extinction and dislocation leave us in doubt about whether we will "live on" in our children and their children, in our groups and organizations, in our works, in our spirituality, or even in nature, which we now know to be vulnerable to our pollutions and our weaponry. It is the loss of faith, I think, in these four modes of symbolic immortality that leads people, especially the young, to plunge— sometimes desperately and sometimes with considerable self-realization—into the mode of experiential transcendence. This very old and classical form of personal quest has had to be discovered anew in the face of doubts about the other four modes. In Chapter 6, I will suggest ways in which much of the personal and cultural experimentation we see around us can be understood in connection with attempts to revitalize the modes of immortality.

In postulating a theory of symbolic immortality on such a grand scale, one must also account for the everyday idea of death, for the sense of *mortality* that develops over the course of a lifetime. Freud's notion of the death instinct is unacceptable. The idea of an instinct that aims toward death could in fact be viewed as a contradiction in terms in that instinctual forces are in the service of the preservation of life.

Nor is death an adequate goal for life. Yet as is generally the case with Freud when we disagree with him, the concept, whatever its confusions around the instinctual idiom, contains an insight we had best retain concerning the fundamental importance of death for psychological life. Hence, the widespread rejection of the death instinct poses the danger not so much of throwing out the baby with the bath water as perhaps of dispensing with the grim reaper with the scythe.

Freud himself faced death heroically and understood well the dangers involved in denying man's mortality. But Freudian theory, in its insistence that death has no representation in the unconscious, has relegated fear of death to a derivative of fear of castration. Freud also seemed ambivalent about whether to view death and life within a unitary or dualistic perspective. His ultimate instinctual dualism opposed death and life instincts. Yet the notion of life leading inevitably toward death is a unitary vision, and it is this unitary element that I think we should preserve. This unitary perspective would insist upon seeing death as an absolute infringement upon the life of the organism (as opposed to certain contemporary efforts to subdivide death into a number of different categories). In this sense death is an event anticipated, and therefore influential, from the beginning of the life of the organism.

I believe that the representation of death evolves from dim and vague articulation in the young organism's inchoate imagery to sophisticated symbolization in maturity. I rely here in part on Kenneth Boulding's work on the image,[9] in which he has stressed the presence in the organism from the very beginning of some innate tendency or direction which I call an inchoate image. This image is at first simply a direction or physiological "push." But inchoate though it may be, the image includes an *interpretive anticipation of interaction* with the environment. Evidence for the existence of innate imagery can be drawn from two sources; one is ethology and the other is observation of rapid eyeball movements (REM) in sleep studies.

Work in ethology has demonstrated through the study of "releasing mechanisms" the existence of what I am here calling an image. The newborn organism is impelled innately toward certain behavior which is "expected" by the older (nurturing) organisms. When this behavior is encountered it acts as a releasing mechanism for a specific action (such as feeding) on the part of the newborn.

Sleep studies also suggest the presence of images in some form from the beginning of life, even during prenatal experience, that "cause" or at least provide some basis for the rapid eyeball movements observed in various species. Rather than demonstrating the presence of pictorial images, these two areas of research suggest the presence at birth of primordial images as precursors of later more highly articulated imagery.*

In the human being the sequence of this process is from psychological push (or direction of the organism) to pictures of the world (images in the usual sense) to more abstract symbolization. Within this theory of evolving imagery we can understand the elaboration of the inner idea of death from earliest childhood in terms of three subparadigms or polarities. These are: connection versus separation, integrity versus disintegration, and movement versus stasis. The inchoate imagery of the first polarity is expressed in a seeking of connection; this is what John Bowlby has described as "attachment behavior" around sucking, clinging, smiling, crying, and following.[10] The organism actively seeks connection with

---

* The overall question of image formation and the inchoate image is discussed in detail in my forthcoming study, The Broken Connection.

the nurturing or mothering person. First this quest is mainly physiological. Later it is internalized in pictorial image formation, and finally it becomes highly symbolized. The organism's evolution is from simple movement toward the mother to a nurturing relationship with her, and eventually toward connection with other people, with groups, with ideas, with historical forces, etc. Where this striving for connection fails, as it always must in some degree, there is the alternative image of separation, of being cut off. This image of separation forms one precursor for the idea of death.

In a similar way one can look at the idea of integrity versus disintegration. As indicated in the work of Melanie Klein on the infant's fear of annihilation,[11] there is from the beginning some sense of the organism's being threatened with dissolution and disintegration. The terms of this negative image or fear are at first entirely physiological, having to do with physical intactness or deterioration. Over the course of time, however, the maintenance of integrity, though it never loses its physiological reference, comes to assume primarily ethical-psychological dimensions. These more symbolic dimensions take hold concomitantly with the development of a sense of "self." Thus one comes to feel the self disintegrating at moments when one's inner forms and images become inadequate representations of the self–world relationship and inadequate bases for action. Such moments may imply no immediate physical threat to the integrity of the organism.

The third mode, that of movement versus stasis, is the most ignored of the three; but it has great clinical significance and is especially vivid to those who deal with children. An infant held tight and unable to move becomes extremely anxious and uncomfortable. The early meaning of movement is the literal, physiological idea of moving the body or a portion of it from one place to another. Later the meaning of movement takes on symbolic qualities having to do with development, progress and change (or with a specific collectivity in some form of motion). The absence of movement becomes a form of stasis, a deathlike experience closely related to psychic numbing.

One could illustrate in detail the evolution of these polarities over the course of the life cycle. But it is clear that rather early, earlier than is usually assumed, death achieves some kind of conscious meaning. By the age of three, four, and five, children are thinking and talking, however confusedly, about death and dying. And over the course of the next few years something in that process consolidates so that the idea of death is more fundamentally learned and understood. At every developmental level all conflicts exacerbate, and are exacerbated by, these three aspects of what later becomes death anxiety—that is, disintegration, stasis, or separation. These death-linked conflicts take on characteristic form for each developmental stage and reach a climax during adolescence. During young adulthood there occurs a process partly described by Kenneth Keniston around the term "youth"[12] and partly described in my own work around the concept of the "Protean style"[13] (named after the Greek god Proteus, a notorious shape-shifter). I see the continuing search characterizing the Protean style as a constant process of death and rebirth of inner form. The quest is always for images and forms more malleable and inwardly acceptable at this historical moment than are those available from the past. Sometime in early adulthood one moves more fully into the realm of historical action, and one then connects with the modes of symbolic immortality.

Later, in middle adulthood, one becomes impressed that one will indeed die. It becomes apparent that the limitations of physiology and life span will not permit the full accom-

plishment of all one's projects. But even with this fuller recognition of mortality the issues of integrity, connection, and
movement remain salient. Old people approaching death
look back nostalgically over their whole lives. This "life review," as it is sometimes called, has to do with a process of
self-judgment. One examines one's life around issues of integrity, connection and movement, and searches for evidence
of relationship to the modes of symbolic immortality.

How do these principles apply in mental disturbance? Psychiatrists have turned away from death, as has our whole culture, and there has been little appreciation of the importance
of death anxiety in the precipitation of psychological disorder. I want to suggest the clinical applicability of this paradigm of death and the continuity of life for various categories
of psychopathology.

What I am here calling the sense of immortality is close to
what Erik Erikson calls basic trust.[14] Erikson emphasizes the
issue of basic trust as the earliest developmental crisis, and
he sees the legacy of this earliest time as having vital importance for adulthood. But the establishment of trust itself involves confidence in the integrity, connection, and movement
of life, prerequisites for a viable form of symbolic immortality. Where this confidence collapses psychological impairment ensues.

The principle of impaired death imagery—or, more accurately, of impaired imagery of death and the continuity of
life—is a unitary theme around which mental illness can be
described and in some degree understood. I see this kind of
impairment as being involved in the etiology of mental illness but not as causative in the nineteenth-century sense of a
single cause bringing about one specific effect. Rather, impaired death imagery is at the center of a constellation of

forms, each of which is of some importance for the overall process we call mental disturbance. Here I would point to three relevant issues central to the process of mental illness. The first is death anxiety, which evolves in relation to the three polarities I have described. The second is psychic numbing, which I see as a process of desymbolization and deformation. The image which accompanies psychic numbing is that "if I feel nothing, then death does not exist; therefore I need not feel anxious about death either actually or symbolically; I am invulnerable." A third principle is what I call "suspicion of counterfeit nurturance." This is the idea that if death exists, then life is counterfeit. Offers of aid and support are mistrusted and even despised, because these serve as reminders of one's vulnerability and mortality. Ionesco's question "Why was I born if it wasn't forever?" illustrates the relation of this theme to the quest for immortality. But it is a very old question.

Death anxiety can be seen as a signal of threat to the organism, threat now understood as disintegration, stasis or separation. All anxiety relates to these equivalents of death imagery, and guilt too is generated insofar as one makes oneself "responsible" for these processes. In Chapter 4 I distinguish between static (either numbed or self-lacerating) and animating guilt, and emphasize the importance of the latter in the process of self-transformation.[15]

One can take as a model for much of neurosis the syndrome which used to be called "traumatic neurosis" or "war neurosis." It is generally described as involving the continuous reliving of the unconscious conflicts aroused by the traumatic situation. More recently, emphasis has been placed on imagery of death aroused by the trauma, rather than the trauma *per se*. Thus the syndrome has been called by some observers "death anxiety neurosis."[16] I see this process in terms of the psychology of the survivor as I have elaborated that psychology in my work on Hiroshima and more recently with antiwar veterans. My belief is that survivor conflicts emerge from and apply to everyday psychological experience as well. When one "outlives" something or someone, and there are of course many large and small survivals in anyone's life, the specter of premature death becomes vivid. Simultaneously one begins to feel what I came to call in my Hiroshima work "guilt over survival priority." This is the notion that one's life was purchased at the cost of another's, that one was able to survive *because* someone else died. This is a classical survivor process and is very much involved in traumatic neurosis. In describing traumatic neurosis, earlier observers spoke of "ego contraction."[17] That is close to what I call psychic numbing, also very marked in the survivor syndrome and in neurosis in general.

A great number of writers (including Stekel, Rank, Horney, and Tillich) have emphasized patterns closely resembling psychic numbing as the essence of neurosis. Stekel, in 1908, spoke of neurotics who "die every day" and who "play the game of dying."[18] Otto Rank referred to the neurotic's "constant restriction of life," because "he refuses the loan (life) in order to avoid the payment of the debt (death)."[19] The neurotic thus seeks to defend himself against stimuli in a way Freud described in a little-known passage in *Civilization and Its Discontents*. Freud observed:

> No matter how much we may shrink with horror from certain situations—of a galley slave in antiquity, of a peasant during the Thirty Years' War, of a victim of the Holy Inquisition, of a Jew awaiting a pogrom—it is nevertheless impossible for us to feel our way into such people, to divine the changes which original obtuseness of mind, a gradual stupefying process, the cessation of expectations and cruder or

more refined methods of narcotization have produced upon their receptivity to sensations of pleasure and unpleasure. Moreover, in the case of the most extreme possibility of suffering, special mental protective devices are brought into operation.[20]

It is strange that Freud turned away from his own argument at this point and concluded that it was "unprofitable to pursue this aspect of the problem any further." For that argument contained the core of the idea of psychic numbing in extreme situations. The holocausts described by Freud have become almost a norm, a model for our times. But in lesser degree, what Freud called narcotization and I am calling psychic numbing is associated with the individual "holocausts" and survivals around which neurosis takes shape.

One can now begin to make some preliminary but still quite specific statements about the significance of these struggles around death imagery for the classical psychiatric syndromes. I am exploring these relationships more fully in work in progress,[21] and my hope is that others will as well.

If we view neurosis in general as an expression of psychic numbing—constriction of the self and diminished capacity for experience—we can see in depression specific examples of impaired mourning, impaired symbolization, and the impaired formulation of the survivor. Where a recognized loss triggers the process, as in reactive depression, the depressed person acts very much like a survivor, and psychic numbing becomes very prominent. Such people often express the feeling that a part of them has died, and that they "killed" the other person in some symbolic way by failing to sustain the other's life with needed support, help, and nurturance. The idea of either having killed the other person or having purchased one's own life at the cost of another's is fundamental. Such feelings are also related to Freud's explanation of guilt, in that earlier ambivalent feelings toward the other person included hate and death wishes, which now become attached to the actual loss. The whole issue of grief and its relation to mental disturbance is too complex to examine fully here. As Colin Parkes and others have shown, grief has great importance in the experience of survival and has a causative influence in the mental disturbance, including psychic numbing, and somatic illness that frequently occur in connection with bereavement.[22]

In character disorders, and in the related phenomenon of psychosomatic disorders in which one speaks through the "language of the body," there are lifelong characterological patterns of deadening or numbing of various aspects of the psyche. This numbing may involve moral sensitivity or interpersonal capacities. However the numbing is expressed, there is a situation of meaninglessness and unfulfilled life, in which the defensive psychological structures built up to ward off death anxiety also ward off autonomy and self-understanding.

Turning to hysteria, the "psychic anesthesia" emphasized in early literature suggests the centrality of stasis, deadening, or numbing. Freud's case of Anna O., for example, is properly understood as a mourning reaction.[23] The hysteria followed very quickly upon the death of Anna's father and had much to do with her reaction to that death. Her conception of being alive became altered in such a way that merely to *live* and *feel*—to exist as a sexual being—was dangerous, impermissible, and a violation of an unspoken pact with the dead person. Whether or not there is a mourning reaction directly involved, hysteria tends to involve either this form of stasis or its seeming opposite, exaggerated movement or activity that serves as a similar barrier against feeling and living. These patterns again resemble those I encountered among Hiroshima survivors.

In obsessional neurosis and obsessive-compulsive styles of behavior the stress is upon order and control. One tries to "stop time," to control its flow so as to order existence and block spontaneous expression, which is in turn felt to be threatening and "deadly."

Much of Freudian theory of phobia evolved from the case of Little Hans. In this case Freud interpreted castration fears as being displaced and transformed into a fear of horses—the inner danger being transformed into an external one.[24] But I would say that Little Hans's experience could also be understood in terms of fear of annihilation and separation. His castration fear epitomized but was not the cause of his general death anxiety. Rather than viewing this death anxiety as secondary to castration anxiety, as psychoanalytic literature has done ever since, we do better to reverse our understanding and interpret the castration anxiety as an expression of more general death anxiety.

Finally, I want to turn to psychosis and to an application of this theoretical position to schizophrenia. One is appalled by the degree to which death imagery has been observed in schizophrenic persons without being really incorporated into any conceptual scheme. As with more general psychiatric concern with death, the situation is changing. Harold Searles writes at some length about the problems a schizophrenic person has with the "universal factor of mortality." Searles says that the schizophrenic patient doesn't really believe he or she is living, doesn't feel alive, feels life passing by, and feels stalked by death. Thus the patient employs a variety of techniques to defend against death anxiety, and yet in another sense feels already dead, "having therefore nothing to lose through death."[25] And what Ronald Laing calls the "false self" is very close to what I am calling a numbed or "dead self." Laing goes on to "translate" from what he calls "schizophrenese" and describes "the desire to be dead, the desire for a non-being" as "perhaps the most dangerous desire that can be pursued." The "state of death-in-life" he sees as both a response to "the primary guilt of having no right to life in the first place, and hence of being entitled at most only to a dead life," and "probably the most extreme defensive posture that can be adopted," in which, "being dead, one cannot die, and one cannot kill."[26] What Searles and Laing describe in schizophrenics is directly reminiscent of the process I observed among survivors in Hiroshima, and is similar to the *Musselmanner* phenomenon that occurred in Nazi concentration camps: so extreme was the state of psychic numbing that, as one observer put it, "one hesitates to call their death death."[27] These were people who had become robots.

The schizophrenic experiences a pathetic illusion of omnipotence, a despairing mask of pseudo-immortality because he is blocked in the most fundamental way from authentic connection or continuity—from what I have been calling a sense of symbolic immortality. He therefore fantasizes omnipotence and pseudo-immortality. But the productions of the schizophrenic are infused with death: again like the Hiroshima survivors at the time the bomb fell, the person feels dead, views other people as dead, and considers the world dead.

Wynne, Lidz, and others who have studied family process in schizophrenia emphasize the transmission of "meaninglessness, pointlessness, and emptiness," of "irrationality," of "schism and skew."[28] Bateson's "double bind" theory of conflicted messages received by the child also stresses the difficulty faced by the child in establishing a coherent field of meaning.[29] All of these theories represent a transmission of "desymbolized" or "deformed" images, which cannot cohere for the child and which leave him overwhelmed with death anxiety and suspicion of counterfeit nurturance. In the child's experience nurturance is dangerous: he flees from it into isolation, stasis, a "safer death" of his own.

It may require several generations to produce a schizophrenic person. But one can say that, however the inheritance mechanism may operate, whatever the contribution of genetic legacy, the early life of the schizophrenic is flooded with death anxiety, and the result is thought disorder and impairment of reality sense. The schizophrenic's behavior and symptoms represent alternate tendencies of surrender to death anxiety and struggle against it. The near-total suspicion of counterfeit nurturance which characterizes the schizophrenic's emotional life renders psychic numbing more extensive and more enduring than in any other form of psychiatric disturbance. Although one sometimes sees in acute forms of schizophrenia an exaggerated response to stimuli, the general and long-range process is one of profound psychic numbing. To the schizophrenic as to certain survivors of mass holocausts, life is counterfeit, inner death predominant, and biological death unacceptable. Because the schizophrenic's existence has been a series of unabsorbable death immersions and survivals, the schizophrenic ultimately settles for a "devil's bargain": a lifeless life.

The paradigm of death and continuity of life—together with psychoformative and psychohistorical perspectives—can help keep psychiatry and psychoanalysis close to their biological origins without imposing on them an instinctual determinism. The paradigm recognizes the scope of human symbolization and provides a link between human biology and human history, a link essential to make if either is to be sustained.

CHAPTER 3

The Basic Psychological Process:
From Analysis to Formation

In Chapter 2 I described a conception of death and the continuity of life which has become increasingly central to my work. This conception comprises the fundamental perspective in a formative depth-psychological paradigm. In this and the following chapter I want to connect this paradigm to the two earlier paradigms from which it derives, those of Freud and Erikson. I will make comparisons in six areas, and in each I will suggest a sequence rather than a break, a shift rather than a replacement. The sequence will include no more than basic landmarks and themes—some quite familiar and others perhaps newly evident on the basis of a contemporary psychohistorical perspective.

I hope to make explicit some of the connections and divergences between my work and that of Freud and Erikson. In so doing I am deliberately neglecting other work of great importance to my own evolving position and to depth psychology in general: writings of Otto Rank and Melanie Klein on death and continuity; of Carl Jung on the self, symbolization, and dreams; of Harry Stack Sullivan and, more recently,

D. W. Winnicott, R. Fairbairn, and Harry Guntrip on the self and personal relations; of R. D. Laing, Leslie Farber, Rollo May, and their predecessors within the phenomenological perspective; and of Sandor Rado and Abram Kardiner on adaptational and cross-cultural psychodynamics. I choose to limit myself to Freud and Erikson because their paradigms have been central to my own psychological formation, and because the larger principles involved in these two shifts seem to me to have importance for the historical sequence of psychological work in general.

In contrast to the formidable opus of both Freud and Erikson, I am well aware that my own theoretical work is something in the nature of a half-formed suggestion. And while the enterprise requires that I emphasize points of departure from Erikson, his extensive influence on my work will be strongly evident. I claim no lack of passion in my theoretical struggles. But I present this study in a nonpolemical spirit of inquiry and acknowledgment, and in the belief that fidelity to one's mentors lies in the receptive confrontation and imaginative re-creation of their legacy. That legacy, moreover, consists of not only their ideas but their "life stories," and includes that important interface at which individual and historical currents come together in new illumination. In such a precarious effort, then, I seek freedom in continuity and the articulation of much that has long been inchoate.

Prior to examining these three paradigms in a comparative way I want simply to state, for purposes of orientation, what I take to be the fundamental tenets of the formative paradigm. Most important is its stress upon motivation around life (form) and death (formlessness). Central to human experience is the struggle to evoke and preserve the sense of the self as alive, and avoid the sense of the self as dead. All living beings share the struggle to remain alive. But the urge to retain and enlarge the *feeling* of being alive—of vitality—is specifically human, an evolutionary trait of symbolizing mentation that stands at the border of biology and culture. These basic aspirations—remaining alive and retaining the "feeling of life"—suggest the stress in formative theory on imagery and symbolization of human continuity. Struggles for vitality and continuity take place simultaneously at levels that can be called proximate (connection-separation, integrity-disintegration, movement-stasis) and ultimate (symbolic immortality).

This paradigm also stresses continuous transformations of form and meaning in both culturally shared and individual-psychological experience. Within individual psychology the formative or mythic zone of the psyche consists of those core constellations and images that are identified most directly with life–death issues. Threats to this formative zone evoke greatest anxiety, while symbolic transformations around these core areas hold greatest potential for fundamental alterations in the self. When transformations of this fundamental nature can be widely shared, we may begin to speak of the remaking of history. But in the dialectic between individual and history (or cultural history), neither is reducible to the other.

Perhaps only one more thing need be said before beginning to explore the paradigms in detail. A stress on form makes a fundamental requirement on method. A perspective emphasizing pattern and configuration obliges one to recognize that every boundary is also a bridge. Whether one is speaking of the individual in relation to the collectivity or of conscious and unconscious aspects of experience, the emphasis in formative theory is always on continuum and transitional process, rather than on dichotomies and absolute breaks. This emphasis can lend to descriptions and explanations framed in formative terms a fluid, at times amorphous, quality in contrast to the crisp distinctions of classical Freudian theory. Part of the difficulty has to do with the relative novelty of the formative approach; we will become increasingly precise as we learn to use new modes of thought more surely. But I suspect the difference is indicative of more complex understandings of cause and effect and subject–object relationships that have taken hold in all branches of science. These in turn make new theoretical efforts compelling but offer little aid and comfort as we begin rethinking our psychological situation.

The six categories I will explore, in comparing the formative paradigm to those of Freud and Erikson are: the nature of the overall psychological model or "controlling image" of human nature; the basic psychological process; the historical sources of each of the three paradigms; the method and interpretive mode; ideas about dreams, symbols, and imagination; and the approach to history. These categories are somewhat arbitrary but sufficiently fundamental, I believe, to justify themselves.

The Controlling Image

The controlling image is the identifying feature of any psychological paradigm, and contains what we may call the "image-model" of human nature. The controlling image in a theory both determines and is determined by what one chooses to study.

In Freud's case the subject of study was practically everything having to do with the mind. He held to the investigative-scientific credo that nothing human was alien to what has been called his "new microscope." But his most specific subject of study was neurosis, and especially its sexual origins. The "disease" that he, as a physician, confronted was mainly hysteria. His patients were mostly young and middle-aged upper-middle-class Viennese Jews, more women than men, living in the late nineteenth and early twentieth centuries. Struggling to be of help to them and to support himself and his family financially, Freud was able to subsume both of these demands to a more basic investigative impulse, to his early recognition that he had "touched upon one of the great secrets of nature." Freud expressed this sense of himself in his declaration (in a letter to Fliess written on February 1, 1900, in a depressed mood following publication of *The Interpretation of Dreams*), "I am actually not at all a man of science, not an observer, not an experimenter, not a thinker. I am by temperament nothing but a *conquistador*, an adventurer, if you want to translate this term—with all the inquisitiveness, daring, and tenacity characteristic of such a man."[1]

Nonetheless, Freud initiated a clinical-syndrome-oriented, private-practice emphasis that has generally prevailed in psychoanalysis, with frequent neglect of the investigative component. Psychoanalysis can be said to have begun with the case history of Fräulein Anna O., which Freud and Breuer first reported in the form of a "Preliminary Communication" in 1893.[2] Freud's capacity to make a revolutionary beginning at the very point of Breuer's retreat (because of his discomfort at his patient Anna O.'s sexual interest in him) depended upon another aspect of Freud's pursuit of his subject of study: his capacity to include *himself* within it. Freud's justly celebrated self-analysis (mostly in 1897)[3] permitted him to make the link, crucial to the innovator, between personal (subjective) and conceptual (generalizing) struggles. For depth-psychological investigators in particular, this linkage requires articulation. With Freud, that articulation was ingenious, subtle, and highly complex. The heart of Freud's self-analysis, in my judgment, lies not so much in overcoming resistances and repressions and thereby discovering the Oedipus complex, as he and others have explained it. Rather, the breakthrough lies in linking them all—complex, resistances, and repressions, as he perceived them in himself—to analogous (and in principle virtually identical) patterns he could perceive in patients and literary sources. For while insights and barriers to them vary according to the paradigm, *the task of blending self and paradigm in creative conceptualization faces every psychological innovator.* Freud's own dreams, as we know, were his "royal road" to this linkage, and his great early work *The Interpretation of Dreams* (written from 1896 to 1899) its consolidation. To carry through that process of linkage and consolidation, Freud had to take imaginative leaps from his subject of study (hysteria, the case history, his own dreams) to universal principles, leaps that were brilliant, risky, responsible, vulnerable, absurd, and awe-inspiring.

But however complex and subtle his imagination, and however ingenious his capacity for including himself within his own paradigm, *Freud's controlling image* (as suggested in Chapter 1) *remained remarkably clear and consistent: that of instinct (mostly sexual) and defense (mostly repression).* His image-model of the human being is one of a driven creature, bringing to bear a fragile superstructure of civilized reason in the attempt to stem demonic biological forces. That image-model is at the center of everything Freud wrote— about neurosis and psychopathology, dreams and normal psychology, and group process and history. We need not rehearse the long-standing controversy as to whether Freud's concept is best translated (from the German *Trieb*) as "instinct" or as "drive," the latter suggesting greater malleability than the former. (One solution often resorted to is the compromise term "instinctual drive.") In any case, Freud's ideas expressed the nineteenth-century view of instinct as a primal, inherited, organized force, or set of impulses, directed toward specific goals and adaptations. Perhaps only Freud could have converted that seemingly antipsychological perspective into a revolutionary new psychology. He did that, I would claim, by searching out formative principles embedded in the nineteenth-century concept of instinct, thereby (still more paradoxically) setting in motion a depth-psychological vision that by its very logic presses toward undermining if not eliminating the instinctual concept itself, at least in human beings.

A central difficulty in Freud's use of instinct has to do with the physicalistic concept of sexual energy or "libido." Freud and his followers have used that term in different ways but invariably in association with the idea of instinctual energy. When Freud said, "One can either drop the term 'libido' altogether or use it as meaning the same as psychic energy in general,"[4] he was in fact extending it to include *all* instinctual or (synonymous for Freud) psychic energy. In practice the word has not been much associated with energy from the death instinct or its precursor the aggressive instincts, for which the terms "mortido" and "destrudo" have at one time or another been suggested. But the word libido could be so applied, at least in principle, and the distinction is rendered less important by psychoanalytic concepts about the merging of these two forms of instinctual energy. More to the point is Freud's sense of libido as a *quantity* of energy. Even if libido in Freud's understanding of it varied according to one's genetic constitution, and even if many things happened to it over the course of psychological experience during childhood in particular, the clear implication was that a certain amount of libido existed on an organic basis. This quantity of libido had either to be discharged (through sexual or related activity), blocked (by means of repression or other defenses), or converted into nonsexual cultural expressions (through sublimation).

It was libido that made the psychic organism go. This "hydraulic" or "steam-kettle" theory of quantified energy was again consistent with the nineteenth-century world-view, as importantly derived from Newtonian physics. But however ingeniously elaborated, it has led to no end of confusion, epitomized by (but by no means limited to) the further literalization of Freud's concept of quantifiable libido in Wilhelm Reich's concept of enclosable and curative "orgone energy." The essential features of Freud's instinctual theory, including its insistent dualism and reliance on the struggle *against* innate forces, would seem to render it not very promising to the contemporary mind. Yet Freud managed to extend it, humanely and brilliantly, beyond its mechanistic origins into subtle dimensions of meaning, failure, aspiration, and tragedy.

As one, in his own word, "educated" by the early psychoanalytic movement, Erikson also draws heavily upon his extensive clinical experience as a psychoanalyst for his subject of study. But there are several significant shifts in emphasis. For one thing, he started out as a child analyst (partly because that was somehow considered appropriate for a nonphysician, and partly, no doubt, because of a personal inclination of this stepson of a pediatrician who had come to psychoanalysis via a teaching position in a school for young children[5])—which, in any case, contributed to his early preoccupation with the life cycle. More than that, he became an exile at the same time he became a psychoanalyst, leaving Europe in his mid-thirties upon completing his training. Thus his subsequent elaboration of identity theory was much influenced and deepened by his concentration upon work with adolescents and young adults in California and in Stockbridge, which may itself be viewed as both cause and effect of his life-cycle focus. By his mid-fifties he had given up almost all clinical work to concentrate on his writing—upon elaborating his new paradigm, I would say. Significantly, his two great "case histories" (or "life histories," as he prefers to call them) have not been those of patients or analysands but of Martin Luther and Mohandas Gandhi, whose lives he could call forth to demonstrate, perhaps for the first time, depth-psychological relationships between "life history and history."[6]

Erikson too includes himself in his subject of study. He does so not by reporting his own dreams but by means of a highly personal voice throughout his writing, and an increasing willingness to make his subjective responses part of the data and, equally, part of his conceptual structure.[7] This "disciplined subjectivity," as he and others have called it, culminates in an especially valuable autobiographical essay in which he juxtaposes his earlier life struggles with the development of identity theory.[8] In his choice of subject, then, Erikson moves from the clinical to the social and historical, always with both rigor and subjectivity, and always around the controlling image of identity and the life cycle.

Erikson does not reject Freud's image-model but rather incorporates it within a controlling image of his own: that of *identity and the life cycle*.[9] For Erikson the human being is an internal wanderer, clinging midst a variety of threats to hard-won elements of continuity. Instinct and defense are both included and transcended in his systematic elaboration of the struggle for coherence and sameness over the course of individual existence. Erikson thus speaks much less than did Freud of drives and defenses, and much more of *patterns* and *configurations.* On the journey through Erikson's "Eight Ages of Man," the individual still carries Freud's instinctual-dualistic baggage, but the contents are taken out into the environmental fresh (or polluted) air, where they can be subsumed to the complex patternings of the individual mind or (within the psychoanalytic structural divisions of the psychic apparatus) the ego. Erikson's sensitive focus on interrelationship and form goes far toward freeing depth psychology from mechanistic fetters and infusing it with a new vitality.

Erikson does not linger much on instinctual territory, but he does insist upon retaining the concept of instinct. Erikson locates Freud's *Trieb* in English translation as "something between the English 'drive' and 'instinct.'" He goes on to make his own differentiation between the words "instinctive" and "instinctual"—the first pertaining to "an inborn pattern of adaptive competence," the second to "a quantity of drive or drivenness, whether adaptive or not."[10] The distinction, with consistent Eriksonian sensitivity, succeeds in divesting at least one version of the term ("instinctive") of its old imagery of "blind force" and of reclaiming it as an *adaptive configuration.* Yet the other version of the term ("instinctual"), though in most usage no different from the first, retains much of its nineteenth-century sense, including that of quantification. Having made an important clarification and called forth from instinct theory what is potentially formative, Erikson is content to leave the matter in some ambiguity.

That spirit is consistent with his earlier work in which he linked Freud's stages of libido theory to psychosocial dimensions and thereby re-created—one might even say rescued— instinct theory. More recently he has done the same in a linkage of instinct and ritual. In his study of Gandhian nonviolence, Erikson notes ethological work of Julian Huxley and Konrad Lorenz on animals' capacity to curb aggression and avoid killing or injury through their ritual assumption of what we would call roles of victor or vanquished: "One can well see in such ritualization . . . an evolutionary antecedent of man's inborn propensity for a moral inhibition that prevents undue violence; and one could well (and I will) go further and see in Gandhi's Satyagraha the suggestion of a pacific confrontation that may be grounded not only in man's religiosity but also in instinctive patterns already common among some 'brutes.'" In the same vein he goes on to talk about ritual conventions of warfare among certain primitive tribes as "a cultural arrangement somewhere between the instinctual and the instinctive and somewhere also between tribal self-insistence and an intertribal league."

While Erikson's general paradigm of identity and the life cycle locates itself mainly in the psychosocial dimension, an underlying concept of instinct remains crucial to it. "In psychoanalysis [instinct theory] is not expendable," he tells us, though noting that "biologists are about to discard it." Like most contemporary psychoanalysts he rejects the concept of the death instinct and like many he "would hesitate to call aggression an 'instinct.'" Still, he says, "If one abandons the term altogether . . . one neglects the energetic and the driven aspect of man's behavior." Instinct is still inseparable from energy source and "drivenness."

My own two subjects of study—they turn out to be just one —have been holocaust and transformation. The unifying principle is the ordeal of the individual death encounter with its possibilities either for stagnation or for renewal. The Korean War propelled me from psychiatric training, mostly Freudian and entirely clinical, to a confusing world "out there." My first paper dealt with combat pilots, and if my perspectives have since changed radically my subject matter has not. I have returned regularly to studies of "extreme situations," though with increasing concern for historical and ethical dimensions: Chinese thought reform and (later) the Chinese Cultural Revolution, Hiroshima survivors, Vietnam veterans. In all of these, issues of individual and social transformation have been as central as those of holocaust and confrontation with death. And in other studies with young adults, university students in Japan and innovative professionals in the United States, I have focused still more directly on struggles around new psychic combinations and shared aspirations toward change.

I too emerge from a clinical orientation. A psychotherapeutic ethos has been central to my work—in my training, in work with patients, and perhaps most basically in what I like to think of as the healing spirit of my research, most of which has consisted of encounters with human beings under some duress. But that research has involved people I sought out because of their experiences rather than people who sought me out for therapy, and I have from the beginning considered myself more an investigator and explorer (if not a "conquistador") than a therapist.

Also important has been my consistent emphasis on the contemporary, which has permitted me to interview directly those people I have sought to understand. With the exception of my study of the Chinese Cultural Revolution, where the treatment of Mao Tse-tung has elements of psychobiography,[11] my "case studies" are not of great historical figures but of groups of relatively ordinary people rendered extraordinary by certain kinds of psychological and historical experience. Influenced by Erikson's stress on human possibility via conflict, I have also been much interested in what the theologian John Dunne calls the "life story," the individual's selective personal narrative or "myth," and its relationship to the "life history" or re-creation of the individual life by the historian or "psychohistorian." The distinction, though sometimes difficult to make, has important bearing on the question of who brings what to the narrative—as perceived by the person in question, the investigator-writer, and the audience-reader.

In thus moving still further from medical-psychoanalytic structure, I have had to bring to my work new elements of subjectivity that I have been struggling to articulate. A key turning point here was my work in Hiroshima. Early in that study I began to observe in myself a process by which my initial pain, anxiety, and horror became sufficiently ameliorated for me to carry out my investigative function.[12] I thought much about the process of "selective professional numbing" and its relationship to the balance we require between involvement and detachment, or what Martin Buber calls "distance and relation." I came to see the importance of defining the professional observer's personal location or "psychohistorical place," and tried to do that for myself retrospectively with a series of individual essays written over a single decade[13]—and, more recently, in my more active struggles to combine antiwar passions with investigative scrutiny. To carry further this examined subjectivity I have been for some time collecting my own dreams, trying to bring a formative perspective to bear on them in the service of that crucial link between the self of the innovator (or would-be innovator) and the general principles being sought. My work in general presses toward freer expressions of subjectivity and new ways of combining it with investigative rigor.

The controlling image in my work is that of *death and the continuity of life* (as described in Chapter 2).[14] In studying various kinds of individual and collective experience in holocaust and social change, I have been concerned with the

62 : *The Life of the Self*

struggle to maintain and extend life in the face of death. In this sense my controlling image might be more accurately described as the continuity and discontinuity of life, or the continuity of life with death and its psychic precursors. My image-model is one of fluid self-process, close to Guntrip's idea of the "development, disintegration, and re-integration of the Self"[15] as the essence of psychodynamic processes. It is an image-model of the human being as a perpetual "survivor" —first of birth itself, and then of the "holocausts" large and small, personal and collective, that define much of existence— but a survivor capable of growth and change, especially when able to confront and transcend those "holocausts" or their imprints.

In Chapter 2 I outlined the subparadigms of connection-separation, movement-stasis, and integrity-disintegration, through which, from the beginning until the end of life, imagery of continuity and discontinuity is perceived and recast. The concept of symbolic immortality moves outward from the individual and connects the individual to historical flow and cultural projects extending beyond the self. A cardinal principle of the paradigm is that, *at every moment, the self is simultaneously involved with both proximate and "ultimate" matters.** A discussion with my fourteen-year-old son,

* Significantly, Edward O. Wilson, in his description of elementary concepts of sociobiology, uses virtually the same terms. He distinguishes the "proximate causation" of more or less conventional "functional biology" with the "ultimate causation" of "evolutionary biology." He identifies his own work with the latter, and states that the "prime movers of evolution" ("necessities created by the environment: the pressures imposed by weather, predators, and other stressors, and such opportunities as are presented by unfilled living space, new food sources, and accessible mates") influence the directions of genetic evolution through natural selection and are the "ultimate biological causes" that shape anatomy, physiology, and behavior. (Wilson, *Sociobiology: The New Synthesis,* Cambridge, Mass.: Harvard Univ. Press, 1975.) Without attempting a systematic comparison, I would say that not only is Wilson's language similar to my own but that there is an for instance, has bearing on both my immediate feelings toward him around connection and separation (including love and conflict between us) and seemingly more "distant" but equally compelling concerns about my ongoing family (biological or biosocial) connectedness and continuity (or symbolic immortality). Similarly, when a colleague questions one of my concepts, my immediate reactions have to do both with feelings specific to the relationship and personal wound and with my inner questions around the quality and enduring potentiality of my work (or "works").

I do not think the concept of instinct is consistent with the formative perspective. Contemporary biologists have already, as Erikson suggests, either discarded the concept or radically altered it, and there is certainly much to be gained by replacing the concept with a formative one, especially in association with human beings. I described in Chapter 2 the idea of an inchoate image, an anticipatory interpretation of the environment which functions as little more than an overall (organismic) physiological inclination or direction of the newborn. This "thrust" of the organism is toward the nurturing that will keep it intact, connected, and active (in movement). Subsequent motivation remains related to these basic principles of vitality even as they are rendered infinitely more complex by the evolving inner imagery of childhood and adulthood. The struggle then shifts from physiological survival to what is perceived as psychic survival, which is in turn inseparable from form and meaning.

In this context, the word "energy" becomes conceptually confusing. And in the more popular sense, feeling "filled with

---

interesting convergence of ideas. One could, for instance, take my concept of biological immortality, the most basic of the five modes within my "ultimate dimension," and see that as the psychological and symbolic equivalent of Wilson's "ultimate causation" via the prime movers of evolution.

energy" usually refers to intense motivation related to a form of recentering that provides newly experienced meaning. Above all, these psychic processes can never be understood in terms of fixed quantities of energy or power.

Indeed, the very use of the term "energy" as a more or less autonomous element is a legacy of the nineteenth-century world of mechanism. I prefer to speak instead of ordering processes that call forth and direct physiochemical energy or force (also variable rather than fixed, though finite). From this standpoint tendencies toward strength or weakness, toward "energetic interests" or apathy, are attributable not to quantities of instinctual energy but rather to the development over the life cycle of motivating psychic forms, and the interplay of these forms with varied genetic-organismic legacies. I would argue for rescuing the concept of energy from its relatively recent association with mechanism and restoring its original relationship to mind and body (as in such pre-Aristotelian words as *energēs, energos* [active, at work], *ergon* [work, action] and *organon* [tool]). Even in the last meaning, the tool, like the work or "energy," derives from the model of the human organism. Hence the etymological relationship of energy to such words as "dramaturgy," "liturgy," "synergism," and "orgasm." From such a perspective we can also rescue the term "psychic energy" to convey a subjective sense of vitality and wholeness. That is, one *feels* energetic at such moments when one's psychic forms are most exquisitely intact—when one is in a state of maximum "centering" (as we shall explain below). We then reach the point at which the *concept* of motivation joins the *experience* of vitality (or psychic energy). And even this briefest of sketches of work in progress suggests that behavior generally thought to be derived from instinct, such as sexuality and aggression, can be more closely studied and understood in terms of a formative process of mind and body evolving over the life cycle, as part of the overall organismic quest for life and form.

The Basic Psychological Process

Freud's basic psychological process is the clash between instinctual drives (id impulses) and the restraining forces brought to bear on them (ego defenses and developing superego, having to do with the demands and morality of civilized society). The process, then, is *defensive* and *compensatory*. The human being is psychologically created through this struggle to tame, alter, shape, and above all defend against and compensate for these primordial elements. While Freud had no doubts about which contender was the stronger (World War I, he wrote, confirmed the psychoanalytic thesis that "our intellect is a feeble . . . thing, a plaything and tool of our instincts and affects"[16]), it is a gross misunderstanding to label him an irrationalist, as some of his opponents have. The opposite was closer to the truth. Reason, in its Enlightenment definition of rationality, was perhaps his strongest ideal. (Consider his two celebrated statements: "The voice of the intellect is a soft one, but it does not rest until it has gained a hearing"[17] and "Where id was there ego shall be."[18])

Rationality as an ideal, in fact, contributed to the fascination that irrational forces held for him, as well as to his insistence, very much in the spirit of Descartes, on a sharp dichotomy between the irrational and the rational, between "primary" and "secondary" process. According to that dichotomy, the human being is always condemned to a more or less losing struggle against the fundamental power of the irrational. Freud's understanding of that struggle, of fragmentary unconscious impulses, ideas, and images threatening always to overwhelm the conscious mind, reflected what

L. L. Whyte has called the "kinetic atomism" of nineteenth-century science. The individual's attempt to defend against these primordial elements (develop and maintain a more rational psychic organ, the ego) can lead to achievement, to symptoms, or, more characteristically, to both. But even the most distinguished human attainment has the quality of compensation, of substituting for (being a sublimation of) the irrational (mostly sexual) unconscious forces.

Vulnerability in a psychological paradigm includes the central impediment (obstacle) and impairment (mode of dysfunction) to its basic psychological process. For Freud the impediment can be understood as the constellation of repression and resistance. Repression has to do with forgetting, excluding an idea, image, affect, or experience from consciousness, or relegating it to the realm of the unconscious. Most subject to repression are instinctual elements that are in turn related to early-childhood experience. Repression for Freud is paradoxical. As "the cornerstone" of all psychoanalytic insight, repression is both necessary for normal psychological development and the source of every variety of destructive and self-destructive psychopathology. Freud originally placed almost exclusive stress on sexual repression. He later turned his attention to repression of aggression and guilt, both as components of the death instinct; and to the "defusion" or separation of the instincts, with a resulting preponderance of destructive impulses. In Freud's paradigm, then, repression becomes an impediment either when it is exaggerated, "too strong," in which case one loses touch with feeling and experience (as in hysteria and other forms of neurosis), or when it is ineffective, "too weak," causing one to be overwhelmed with instinctual imagery (as in psychosis).

Resistance is inseparable from (in Jones's terms, the ob-

verse of) repression. Resistance (as in the case of a body re-
sisting electric current) suggests an active force in opposition
to a process, in this case that of making unconscious elements
conscious. Resistance thus suggests energy brought forth in
defense of repression and in opposition to insight, especially
that form of insight most needed, such as insight about early
psychosexual development and about unacceptable images
and wishes; that is, insight provided by psychoanalysis. Most
generally, resistance is (again in Jones's term) "a manifestation of the repressing forces,"[19] simultaneous with repression
and, together with repression, part of a single entity. Hence,
insufficient resistance can also be an impediment to the basic
psychological process, as it can be to the psychoanalytic
process in therapy.

The most general impairment in Freud's paradigm is that
of regression or reversion to an earlier state or mode of functioning. Neurotic and psychotic symptoms, though differing
in their relationship to such things as repression, reality, and
the topography of the psyche in general, all express regression to prior stages of sexual (libido) development, as well as
"compromise formations" between the unconscious wish or
fantasy and the defensive-regressive agency. The regressive
process is enhanced by prior fixations, or failure to progress
satisfactorily through particular stages of sexual development. The most severe psychiatric conditions (psychoses and
disabling neuroses) express the most intense and earliest
forms of regression (to, for instance, oral and anal stages,
dominated by primary-process thought), while the regression in milder neurotic conditions is more likely to be less intense and associated more with later libidinal stages (Oedipal,
phallic, and genital, in which more secondary-process thought
is retained).

Generally speaking, then, the central vulnerability in

Freud's basic psychological process has to do with the precariousness of the equilibrium between instinct and defense. Or, one could say, the balance between the life and death instincts is tipped in favor of the latter. The result is susceptibility to breakdown expressed in regression. That vulnerability, moreover, is fed from all directions—from organic tendencies toward overly strong instincts, overly weak defenses, overly strong defenses, or overly weak instincts, or any dysfunctional combination thereof; or from trauma, mostly very early and primarily sexual, which interferes with the development of proper instinctual or defensive function.

Erikson, again characteristically, subsumes Freud's version of psychological process to a more contemporary view of that process. Defensive and compensatory maneuvers occur within specific patterns and configurations, which are in turn increasingly responsible for individual and collective destiny.

This highly important change in emphasis emerges early in Erikson's work. I can remember the deep impression made upon me (in 1950 or 1951, when I was a psychiatric resident) by the passage in *Childhood and Society* explaining how the toddler who becomes aware for the first time that he can walk has acquired not only a skill that can be understood within Freud's stages of psychosexual development, but also a "new status and stature of 'one who can walk' with whatever connotation this happens to have in the co-ordinates of his culture's space-time—be it 'one who will go far,' 'one who will be able to stand on his own feet,' 'one who will be upright,' or 'one who must be watched because he might go too far.' "[20] What I dimly sensed then, and came to recognize more clearly later on, was that Erikson was establishing not only what he called "the beginnings of identity" but also the overriding importance of the evolving configuration of the "I" (whether in the form of self, ego, or identity)—and its relationship to the "we"—over the course of the life cycle. Precisely that principle enabled Erikson to propel psychoanalysis into the more characteristic twentieth-century terrain characterized by Whyte as "ordered structure."[21]

For Erikson, that dysequilibrium between instinct and defense contributes significantly to the more general dysfunction of identity confusion; to the specific vulnerabilities of the life cycle on the way toward adolescent identity formation (mistrust rather than basic trust, shame and doubt rather than autonomy, guilt rather than initiative, inferiority rather than industry, and role confusion rather than identity); and to the later vulnerabilities of adulthood and maturity (isolation rather than intimacy, stagnation rather than generativity, and despair rather than integrity). But while repression and resistance can be important impediments, so can the absence of "confirmation" of identity elements on the part of significant individuals and groups around one. Impediments, that is, are never purely intrapsychic but always psychosocial in ways that are specific to a particular stage in the life cycle. Similarly, while regression is an ever available impairment, Erikson emphasizes the importance of psychosocial "conditions for regression." He is also critical of the use of the word "infantile" to depict regressive and disturbed behavior, emphasizing that dysfunction of this kind cannot be equated with the infant's healthy function in a manner appropriate to its stage in the life cycle.[22]

Underlying the vulnerability of identity itself, however, is the persistent threat of the return of early anxiety—"the individual's unconscious determination never to meet his childhood anxiety face to face again." Since man's "earliest sense of reality was learned by the painful testing of inner and outer goodness and badness," he "remains ready to expect from some enemy, force, or event in the outer world that which, in fact, endangers him from within: from his own angry drives, from his own sense of smallness, and from his own split inner world." Erikson thus tells us that identity can be threatened from virtually any direction, but that its ultimate vulnerability to anxiety (or to what he calls "basic fears") stems directly from its infantile origins.[23]

My own inclination concerning basic psychological process is to press the revolution still further. This requires an explicit rejection of Freud's dichotomy between primary (irrational) and secondary (rational) process, and of his accompanying defensive-compensatory concept. In its place I suggest an increasingly articulated focus on *form per se*. The resulting principle of a *formative* (or psychoformative) *process*, characterized by evolving images and psychic forms, owes much not only to Freud's and especially Erikson's evocation of the formative potential of psychoanalysis, but also to Cassirer and Langer's stress on symbolization and symbolic forms,[24] Whyte's focus on unitary and formative principles,[25] and Kenneth Boulding's broad-ranging concept of the image.[26] Within this approach, configurations do not consist of the fragments of a compensatory-defensive process. Rather, each image and form is understood both as a configuration in itself and as part of a larger configuration. Only by creating, maintaining, and breaking down and re-creating viable form are we capable of experiencing vitality—and in that very sense we may say that form equals life.

The formative process can be understood to take place in terms of the three closely related struggles or "subparadigms" discussed in Chapter 2 in connection with the evolution of symbolization around life and death. Each of these subparadigms—connection-separation, movement-stasis, integrity-disintegration—progresses from physiological inclination to enactment to inner imagery to symbolization (or psychoformation). Each takes shape initially in relation to bodily impulses and physical relationships to sources of nurturance and protection; each issues ultimately in complex adult capacities mediated by symbolization: capacities for participation in love and communal relationships, for moral and ethical commitment, and for maintaining a sense of self that includes symbolic development, growth, and change.

All this depends upon the interrelated capacities for *centering* and *grounding*. While centering has been used in different ways in association with Oriental disciplines and Western phenomenology,[27] I understand it as the ordering of experience by the self along the various dimensions that must be dealt with at any given moment—temporal, spatial, and emotional. On the temporal plane centering consists of bringing to bear upon the immediate encounter older images and forms in ways that can anticipate future encounters. On the spatial plane, centering means unifying immediate (proximate) exposure, including bodily involvement, with "distant" ("ultimate," "abstract," "immortalizing") meanings. A third aspect of centering is that of making discriminations in emotional valence between our most impassioned images and forms (what we call the "core" of the self) and those that are less impassioned and therefore more peripheral. The configuration of images which constitutes the psychic core is unique to each individual. In this sense Jungian archetypes can be confusing in their overgenerality and appearance of preexistent form. Yet we can say that there are consistent core areas of the self around which such images and constellations tend to cluster over the course of the overall life cycle. These include (1) sexuality and personal bonds; (2) learning, working, and making; (3) death, play, and transcendence;

(4) home and place; (5) relationship to society and environment; and (6) nurturance and growth. Though these core areas could be conceptualized somewhat differently, they could not, within a formative perspective, be reduced to the single Freudian "nuclear [Oedipus] complex."

All three levels of ordering (temporal, spatial, and emotional) enable one to feel, in turn, "at the center of things" —to experience a self, one's own, which in turn enables one to experience a "world" in which the self is located.

The self can retain its centeredness only to the degree it has the capacity for decentering, for sufficient detachment from its involvements to be able to make judgments upon events and principles beyond itself. Decentering is necessary to the continual process of altering the existing forms that constitute the self, and to applying those forms to new encounters in ways that make possible new kinds of psychic experience. In decentering there is a partial suspension of close integration in temporal, spatial, and emotional planes, with anticipation of new integrations of a more inclusive kind. The absence of decentering renders the self static, devoid of new content, while absence of centering is associated with inability to connect new experience with viable inner forms. If the self cannot achieve a centering-decentering balance it is unable either to consolidate or to evolve, experience becomes less vivid, and the capacity for ethical conviction (as opposed to moralistic reiteration) diminishes. Centering and decentering, then, are part of a common dialectic, each dependent upon the capacity for grounding.

Grounding in turn is the relationship of the self to its own history, individual and collective, as well as to its biology. Ordinary grounding permits the decentering—separation or alteration of the existing involvements of the self—necessary for growth and change. Decentering inevitably involves the possibility that the self will become *uncentered*, will not co-here and will be unable to make the symbolic transformations necessary to assimilate new experience. Every movement away from centeredness, every encounter with significant novelty (significant in terms of its departure from preexistent inner form), entails anxiety and risk, often guilt, rage, and a sense of inner chaos. Where there is grounding, decentering can exist in healthy tension with centering, and its accompanying pain and confusion can be experienced in the service of *recentering*—achieving a new mode of still-flexible ordering. Where there is no such equilibrium, both centering and decentering are inevitably impaired, and uncentering becomes a perpetual threat.

For instance, the "egocentricity" that Lidz and others ascribe to the schizophrenic person involves a defect not only in centering (profound confusion in spatial, temporal, and valencing dimensions of the self) but also in decentering (inability to separate oneself sufficiently from inner concerns to gain perspective on patterns outside the self). His ideas can be highly imaginative but "ungrounded" (insufficiently anchored in individual experience). We may contrast with this the situation of the young adult innovators (from the group of "radical" or innovative young professionals Eric Olson and I are studying) whose capacity to innovate stems from their *grounded imagination,* from imagery that includes contradictions and paradoxes but nonetheless takes its roots in their individual psychic forms. That imagery may be no less "wild" than that of the schizophrenic person, but, unlike the latter, is related to a functional tension between centering and decentering. That tension encompasses much of psychological experience, of what I call self-process. Conceptualizing in this way, self-process contrasts sharply with the relatively unchanging "intact ego" in Freud's paradigm and helps us to move beyond some of the ambiguities surrounding "sameness" and change in Erikson's identity theory. The centering-decentering-recentering process may entail continuity without sameness—the viable ordering of temporal and spatial dimensions and of emotional valence, even as the content of images and forms undergoes significant alteration.

The same concept of formative process also provides a link to the insights of mystical experiences, with its stress upon oneness and unification; and to related psychological views (those of Brown and Laing, for instance) stressing liberation by means of "losing" or surrendering the self. One need not, as Laing and Brown seem at times to imply, eliminate the self once and for all. Rather, one can (in terms close to those of the Gospels) by "losing the self" (radical uncentering) regain (or experience for the first time) a more centered self. A fluid centering-decentering equilibrium, that is, can open one to experiential transcendence; and experiential transcendence can greatly contribute to both components of that equilibrium. In that sense, transcendent or "peak" experiences epitomize the combination of ordering and flexibility ideally present in the "ordinary" flow of psychological experience.

A basic tenet of the formative process is that in human mentation we receive no perceptions or stimuli nakedly, but inwardly re-create each exposure or encounter in our ongoing struggle toward form. That re-creation is always retrospective as well as prospective in ways already suggested, but must be understood in terms of its own timing, in terms of the present.* The *image* is the more immediate link between nervous system and environment. It suggests a picture,

* This formulation is consistent not only with Cassirer and Langer, but also with concepts of "representation" expressed by Piaget in essentially cognitive terms and by many engaged in brain research in essentially neurophysiological terms.

though the word can be extended to imply an anticipatory interpretation of the environment (or "schema for enactment," in Olson's term). "Form" (or constellation) in this sense has some of the characteristics of a "complex," contains many images, and tends to be relatively more enduring than most images. Being more highly symbolized, it possesses greater structure and contour evolved from more elaborate psychic re-creation. Thus employed, the term "form" has the philosophical meaning of "the essence of something as opposed to its matter" (*Oxford English Dictionary*), rather than the seemingly opposite popular meaning of appearance as opposed to content or reality.

For example, I have fleeting (and not so fleeting) images—as well as sustained and complex symbolized forms—having to do with people around me (my wife, children, friends, colleagues), with my work (my research, teaching, theoretical concepts), my sexuality, my death (the end of "me" and my struggle for continuity with ideas and images that can live beyond that end), and with my relationship to social and political issues. Each of these images and forms both interconnects with the others and has some autonomy. They are specific to me, but they also connect with those held by others, so that we can speak of shared imagery, forms, and themes. They are not reducible to a single form (such as the Oedipus complex). Rather, each is a relatively ordered re-creation of all that I have experienced in that realm, bodily and psychically. Each represents my way of feeling and knowing that aspect of my existence, and is in turn inseparable from the remaining psychic forms that make up the overall constellation of my "self" (or self-process), which is in turn my way of symbolizing (re-creating in a relatively ordered way) my sense of my own organism (or the organism bearing my name).

When I sought to understand responses of either atomic-bomb victims in Hiroshima or Vietnam veterans, over time, to their holocaust and survival, I focused on neither their drives and defenses nor their drive-related identity configuration (though the latter came much closer), but on the images and forms taking shape within them in relationship to the death encounter itself, their prior lives, and their subsequent struggles. With Hiroshima survivors, these images and forms had to do with the bomb and death, ultimate annihilation, early religious and cultural experience, feelings toward wartime leaders, toward the United States as perpetrator, occupier, democratic source, and hydrogen-bomb maker, toward family, work, and life in their city and in postwar Japan, and toward me as an American and a person of professional standing (doctor, professor, psychiatrist). What mattered was their overall ordering (or "formulation") of all these elements in ways that contributed to and interfered with their recovery and revitalization.[28] With Vietnam veterans, significant images and forms concerned dying in Vietnam—buddies killed, dead Vietnamese, or their own imagined death—prior experiences around masculinity, family ethos, and patriotism, as well as changing views of love, integrity, autonomy, and relationship to various groups, including one's nation.[29] My interpretations of these patterns, moreover, depended upon my way of viewing them—that is, upon my own images and forms, both those particular to Hiroshima and Vietnam and those having a more indirect bearing upon those experiences.

Much remains to be investigated concerning such basic questions as the virtual equivalence of form and meaning, the relationship between form and awareness (or "consciousness"), and the priority among forms in their determinative significance. But we can say now that the formative perspective permits us to raise fundamental questions about a number of misleading dichotomies—not only that of the rational versus the irrational, but also consciousness versus the unconscious,* the manifest versus the latent, emotion versus cognition, and stability versus change. Concerning the last, we may speak instead of a dialectical relationship between con-

---

* I agree with Whyte when he states: "It may be wrong to think of two *realms* which interact, called the conscious and the unconscious, or even of two contrasted kinds of mental process, conscious and unconscious, each causally self-contained until it hands over to the other. There may exist, as I believe, a single realm of mental processes, continuous and mainly unconscious, of which only certain transitory aspects or phases are accessible to immediate conscious attention." Whyte goes on to suggest several principles for a new mental science, including the assumption "that a unified theory is possible, and lies ahead, in which 'material' and 'mental,' 'conscious' and 'unconscious,' aspects will be derivable as related components of one primary system of ideas . . ."; that "this future theory of mental processes will constitute a special application of a more general theory of organism, and this in turn of a still more general theory of the transformations of partly ordered complex systems, based on a universal postulate that in isolable systems disorder tends to decrease" and that "any process illustrating it will be called *ordering* or *formative*"; that "most organisms may be described as hierarchical systems of ordering processes" and " 'mental' processes are the expression of an ordering tendency evident *both* in a complete physiological description of the processes of the central nervous system and the brain, *and* in a subjective description of directly experienced states." Whyte understands "conscious" to mean "*directly present in awareness*" and "unconscious" to mean "*all mental processes except those discrete aspects or brief phases that enter awareness as they occur* . . . [including] organic or personal tendencies or needs, memories, processes of mimicry, emotions, motive, intentions, policies, beliefs, assumptions, thoughts, or dishonesties."

Like Susanne Langer he objects to the use of "conscious" and "unconscious" in noun forms, and he states: "A single integrated transformation proceeds in a single organ: the mind-brain." He states the hypothesis that "*conscious aspects of mental processes are distinctions affecting the momentarily dominant ordering processes*" and that "*the content of awareness is the tension of a contrast.*" And as a program of research he suggests to "discover the meaning of 'dominant' in terms of structure and function"; and also "how contrasts can be ordered," since "we are definitely conscious at any one moment only of a few relatively stable contrasts, and unconscious of the vast changing complexity of which they form part"—since, that is, "the senses discriminate; the (unconscious) mind orders."[30]

tinuity and re-creation so that, formatively speaking, everything connects with what has gone on before, and nothing stays exactly the same. What we call stability may well depend precisely upon degrees of change, just as transformation may depend upon continuity with the past. My use of the terms "self-process" and "Protean style" reflects my efforts to redress the contemporary conceptual imbalance between exaggerated stress on *enduring* infantile (pathological) patterns and *stable* (healthy) identity, on the one hand, and insufficient recognition of the multiplicity of seemingly divergent images and forms (the collage pattern of the mind) and their perceptual re-creation or transformation, on the other.

In my work the impediment to the basic psychological process consists either of *blocked* image-form interaction, *absence* of required images or forms, or deformation of some kind. Impediment and impairment converge around loss of grounding with disruption of both centering and decentering, and ultimately desymbolization. Impaired grounding involves all three dimensions (temporal, spatial, and emotional valence) but generally one more than the others. It may manifest itself, for instance, in the static embrace of old forms to the exclusion of immediate encounter and of prospective imagery (in which case we can say that temporal centering is impaired and decentering is virtually absent). Or it may imply an exaggerated pragmatism with near-total preoccupation with immediate struggles to the exclusion of larger principles (impaired spatial centering and insufficient decentering). Or the manifestation may be in a seemingly reversed (but related) situation, as often prevails in late adolescence, in which transcendent visions exclude immediate involvements (decentering here, though exaggerated, is no less impaired than is spacial centering). Any of these is likely to be associated with distortion or loss of focus in emotional valence, so that no psychic form or group of forms becomes more central than others. Impaired grounding inevitably leads to desymbolization, a state in which one can no longer re-create (give form to or symbolize) at least certain kinds of experience. Loss of centering and desymbolization are likely to follow upon extremely intense imagery of separation, disintegration, and stasis in a losing struggle to give psychic form to internal and external environments.

The impairment or dysfunction around loss of grounding and desymbolization is that of widespread desensitization or psychic numbing. The impairment is characterized by various degrees of inability to feel and by gaps between knowledge and feeling. Its subjective experience need not be only that of apathy or "deadening," but can take the form of anger or rage (at those seen as responsible for the "killing" of feeling or meaning) or even guilt or shame (where one takes on the responsibility for the "murder"). Psychic numbing, as the central impairment within the formative process, can occur in association with the entire gamut of survivor experience, including that of everyday life. It must always be understood in terms of the present, though it too can have significant early sources in inadequately formulated childhood experience of separation, stasis, and disintegration. Numbing can thus be juxtaposed with the general human mode of "feeling" (in Langer's usage, cognitive as well as emotive, and inseparable from symbolization itself), and is the immediate expression of impaired life–death balance. In this broad usage we can speak of the existence of psychic numbing even in situations (such as the acute schizophrenic process) of "over-inclusion" of stimuli, in which the person is bombarded with unmanageable images and emotions and seems, if anything, to "feel too much." For the "bombardment" itself can be seen as a struggle against the underlying, more basic impairment to symbolization and to feeling.

Psychic numbing can be understood to exist along a continuum. The most extreme form is related to either massive external holocaust or individual-internal equivalents of the kinds mentioned; in-between forms have to do with technological distancing and bureaucratizing of human relations, and with related forms of the numbing of everyday life. The constructive end of the continuum includes creative modes of selective perception, or what I have called partial professional numbing—that of the surgeon who operates the more skillfully for not permitting himself to feel the potential consequences of failure, the pilot who lands his plane more safely by focusing on technical details rather than on the beauties of the sunset, or the artist who avoids certain kinds of imagery and feeling in order to give fuller expression to those he has chosen to re-create. The two ends of the continuum are of course very different. The first pole suggests breakdown of the formative process, or at the very least some impairment and desymbolization in response to what is perceived as a threat to physical or psychic existence. The other pole suggests an enhanced capacity for function and symbolization, within which whatever internal threat exists becomes transmitted and at least managed. Psychic numbing, then, is by no means always a bad thing. But I believe it has so expanded and taken on such malignant forms—not only around the technology of destruction but also around the technicization of human arrangements—that we do well to characterize our era as the age of numbing.[31]

In recognizing this continuum we can begin to grasp the subtle relationships between achievement and desensitization, and the overall vulnerability of the formative process. That vulnerability has to do with the pervasive fragility of our images and forms around the continuity of life. More than that, we may see in our present historical moment a radical imbalance between unacceptable death and life continuity. We are haunted by imagery of total annihilation that further undermines our already strained faith in unending connection with past and future. I have suggested that such a situation can give rise to potentially transformative, if risky, modes of psychological experiment or of "Proteanism." It is precisely the vast sense of collective "deadness" which that Proteanism—and, in fact, every expression of experiential or political radicalism—seeks to break out of.[32]

Within this paradigm, absurd death and the discontinuity of life replace repressed and resisted sexuality and identity conflict as the major source of our psychological impairments. The result is not so much a problem of relegating unacceptable ideas to the unconscious, or the experience of identity confusion. The more basic difficulty is the impaired capacity to feel and to give inner order to experience in general.

CHAPTER 4

History and Imagination

Historical Sources of the Three Paradigms

The personal and collective historical sources of anyone's work defy summarization. Yet they are crucial to whatever shift in paradigm that work engenders. With Freud I would emphasize at least four categories of influence. Freud inherited from Renaissance and eighteenth-century Enlightenment thinkers a stress on individual self-realization and a human-centered focus in the quest for truth. He was influenced by certain strands of German Romanticism, especially Goethe, which he seems to have blended with Jewish Kabbalistic and Talmudic influences. From nineteenth-century science Freud acquired a stress on positivism and a mechanistic world-view which often contradicted and compensated for the more imaginative aspects of his psychological thought and method. Finally, Freud was affected by various late nineteenth-century forms of repression, specifically Viennese and broadly European—political repression (toward liberals and dissenters of any kind), religious-ethnic (toward Jews), and, above all, sexual (toward erotic feelings, images, and acts). Freud incorporated all of these elements into his individual history. In his humane scientism, romantic skepticism, finely reasoned spirituality, and muted sexuality, he was very much a child of his age, though a very special one. To say that the last, the muted sexuality, was intrinsic to his insistence on the sexual origin of the neuroses is not to dismiss that theory as "psychologically caused." It is rather to emphasize the interaction of personal and collective conflict in determining one's subject of study and energizing its investigation.[1] The extraordinarily intense repression of sexual feeling in late-Victorian middle-class society (not only in Vienna, of course) had become so extreme that it threatened to tear that society apart at its sensual and affective seams. In connection with the repression itself and its accompanying hypocrisies, "something had to give." More mysterious is the source of Freud's capacity for transmuting conflict shared at that individual-collective interface into an original and newly illuminating vision.

With Erikson, born in 1902, the historical scene shifts.[2] His adolescence coincided with World War I, a fundamental historical turning point that can be said to have ended Enlightenment aspirations. His early adult life coincided with postwar disillusionment and took a semistructured (Germanic) cultural form of wandering and search. Hitlerism appeared about the time of his psychoanalytic training, and "my graduation coincided with my emigration from Europe." That emigration to the United States had to do with Hitler but also with the need to get away from the already suffocating atmosphere (at least for Erikson) of the Viennese psychoanalytic circle of the early 1930s. The decision to move was no doubt also influenced by Erikson's marriage to an American woman who was a teacher with him in the school for the children of those in analysis.

Erikson is half-Jewish, and was raised as a Jew. His intellectual and professional formation took place midst a history, especially for Jews in the professions, dominated by themes of forced emigration, exile, and threats to life and to historical continuity. The holocausts of World War II had great impact upon him, personally and professionally, but more as an intensification of already existing inclinations than as newly formative influences.

Erikson's multifaceted early personal history enhanced his sensitivity to the dislocations of his era: his father (whom he never knew) and his mother both Danish, she also Jewish, his stepfather a German-Jewish pediatrician; his German childhood with its complicated admixtures of German-Danish and (again his words) "Jew-Goy" conflicts; his learning only in early adolescence that he was a "stepson," a role (or, as he was later to call it, identity fragment) that was to stay with him; his rebellion against his bourgeois background and wanderings through Europe as an "artist without a profession"; his being "adopted" (as he put it), this time by the psychoanalytic movement that was to provide him his only professional certification (he had no formal education beyond the *Gymnasium*); and his later professional wanderings through the various geographical areas and intellectual ferments of the United States of the mid-twentieth century. Given his extraordinary individual gifts (a very big "given," to be sure), who could be better prepared to explore the vicissitudes of identity and continuity, and to pursue—radically extend—the configurational possibilities of psychoanalysis and of the life cycle in general?

Determining one's own historical sources is still more difficult. Thinking back on these matters, I am struck by the strong personal importance for me of psychohistorical dislocation—the breakdown and impaired viability of cultural landmarks, of symbols, beliefs, and institutions. In such a context life takes shape in the absence of psychic or communal plan. From that perspective, the Depression and World War II affected me profoundly in psychologically and intellectually formative ways that are by no means fully clear to me.

I suspect that the Depression, from 1929 through the mid-thirties, brought about extensive internalization of the cycle of "boom and bust," through processes we have hardly begun to address. My earliest specific memory of the Depression has to do with the election of 1932, when I was six years old. But I have images from well before that of a precipitous drop in family status, necessitating our moving to a poorer neighborhood where we could be taken in by nurturing "foreign" grandparents. I recall also the ambivalent swings on the part of my parents between loving belief in the magnificent country that had enabled them, members of the first American-born generation of their Russian-Jewish immigrant clans, to rise from real poverty to middle-class comfort, and deep-seated mistrust of America's claim to virtue. That mistrust was accompanied by a sense of imminent threat that had to do with being Jews in a Gentile society, the offspring of immigrants, economically vulnerable, and also with having absorbed at least fragmentary elements of the Marxist imagery that permeated much of the literate Jewish life of that time.

But overriding that ambivalence was my father's personal myth of American emergence: the poor, bright Jewish boy surviving, mostly through cunning, a childhood on New York's tough (but culturally rich) Lower East Side, his intelligence and ingenuity recognized by sympathetic teachers who helped him attain privileged passage through Townsend Harris Hall (then an elite free high school) and finally City College, at that time a center of mostly Jewish excellence and a stepping-off point for successful forays into American society. That myth was sufficiently grounded in actuality to provide a basis for his adult pride as well as for many of his complexities and contradictions. A successful small business-man, he read Marx and Freud in his youth, revered Roosevelt, traded sharply, considered our economic system "unscien-tific," and was a staunch lifelong advocate and nurturer—of City College and free education, a wide circle of friends and relatives of similar backgrounds, and most of all his immedi-ate family.

Through the haze of father–son conflict, he expressed to-ward me a particularly dedicated and loving version of the immigrant Jewish father's impulse to help his son get to places he himself could never reach. I was imbued, I now realize, with a strong sense of the possibilities for individual and social transformation. But the other side of the message was the fragility of everything, especially for Jews. We were to be deeply grateful, since "only in America" could we be treated so well and protected from the ultimate threat that loomed "out there" (mostly in the form of Hitler as destroyer, buffoon, evil incarnate, and fantasy target for our childhood games of violence). We had to be more on our toes, more knowledgeable than others, and yet in our own way (and with a certain amount of frightened disdain for other Jews who seemed "too Jewish") as American as anyone else. The mass murder of Jews seemed both distant and close, shocking and not entirely unexpected, part of an earlier process. Much later a wise friend suggested to me that my Hiroshima work was my path, as a Jew, to the death-camp experience. Of course neither of these holocausts is as yet psychologically absorbed or even absorbable. For me, as for others, they joined with much earlier impressions of a world full of threatening obscurities, a world without clear foundation, infinitely malleable and subject at any moment to apocalypse.

I came to psychiatry still very young, having been encouraged by my parents (again not uncharacteristically) to "skip" terms and school years when given the opportunity by my high academic standing. My education was further accelerated by World War II, so that I graduated from medical school in 1948 at the age of twenty-two and became a psychiatric resident at twenty-three. Psychiatry did not seem to me a means of personal or collective salvation, but I did see it as a way of getting some hold on the slippery fragments of existence and as a precious intellectual oasis within medicine. By that time psychoanalysis had gained its hegemony over most of the major psychiatric departments, and the Freudian–neo-Freudian struggles had lost much of their verve. One could read Freud, Kardiner, Fromm, Erikson, Alexander, and Zilboorg, all with great profit. And I did not feel it very strange to absorb and raise heretical questions toward the Freudian teachings of my psychiatric residency at the Downstate Medical Center in Brooklyn, and then do the same during the more open but less structured neo-Freudian (mostly Sullivanian) exposure I received during my subsequent research affiliation with the Washington School of psychiatry.

None of this, of course, can fully "explain" why, when required to join the military and sent to Japan (I had asked for Paris) as an Air Force psychiatrist during the Korean War, I plunged into a series of involvements with East Asia and struggled toward becoming a new kind of psychiatrist. I have no doubt, however, about the formative influence of this overall exposure to a wide variety of personal and collective images of annihilation and renewal.

Method and Interpretive Mode

Questions of method are closely related to issues discussed in Chapter 3 in connection with controlling image. The method evolved in any paradigm depends both upon prior methods associated with earlier paradigms and upon departures from these brought about by a quest for a different kind of information and influence. Suspecting that his hysterical patients were suppressing ideas and emotions in ways that caused neurosis, Freud abandoned as useless the electrotherapy of his time for the psychoanalytic arrangement of a prone patient speaking to an invisible therapist. Seeking then to overcome the limitations of hypnosis (patients being refractory to it or dependent for improvement on the immediate authoritarian influence of the therapist), Freud evolved an in-between technique of "concentration." In this method the therapist pressed the patient's forehead and urged the patient to recall memories associated with a particular symptom. Finally, Freud settled upon free association.[3] What he groped toward as a means of transcending the limitations of a prior method thus became his revolutionary instrument.

A central issue, however, for the method of free association is the sorting out of unlimited psychic elements, and the inevitable influence of the therapist-investigator's prior assumptions and world-view not only on the ordering-interpretive process but on the content and flow of the associations themselves. While Freud was not without some understanding of these problems, he was impelled by the innovator's impulse toward pressing his method to the outer borders of its possibilities while seeing much of the world through its special prism. That innovative excess, necessary to discovery, tends to be literalized by followers. In consolidating the paradigm they all too often enshrine the method, even at those points of its overextension.

Freud's interpretive mode is expressed in the name he gave the discipline he created. Analysis, according to *The Oxford English Dictionary*, means "the resolution or breaking up of anything complex into its various simple elements, the opposite process to synthesis." The Greek derivatives *analusis* and *analuein* mean respectively a releasing and to undo—the latter further reducible to *ana,* or back, and *luein,* to loosen. So the sense of the word is: to go back to the component parts of an entity in order to loosen and undo them from one another and from the manifestations of the whole.

At the time Freud invoked it, the word "analysis" had wide currency in mathematics, where it meant proving a proposition by resolving it into similar propositions already proved, or resolving problems by reducing them to equations; in chemistry, where it meant resolution of a chemical compound into its constituent elements; and in optics, where it meant the breaking down of light into prismatic constituents. On the basis of Freud's tendency to take on the terminology of the physics of his day, we may suspect that this last form of usage—perhaps even the specific optical example of light being analyzed by a prism—was Freud's model of his approach to the psyche.

The principle of analysis, of course, is as old as Western science, perhaps even Western thought. But Freud came to it via the particular stress of nineteenth-century science upon understanding the mechanism of things by reducing them to their component parts. Inseparable from that principle of analysis was the intense and specific focus upon cause and effect. Thus Freud's earliest use of the words "analysis" and "analyze" had the double meaning of intellectual interpretation via breakdown, on the one hand, and specific form of therapy, on the other. Freud and Breuer first thought of their new therapeutic approach as a form of catharsis. But once repression became "the cornerstone of our understanding of a neurosis," as Freud explained years later, the aim of therapy had to be seen as no longer "to 'abreact' an affect which had got onto the wrong lines." Rather, the aim of the new technique was "to uncover repressions and replace them by acts of judgment which might result either in the accepting or in the condemning of what had formerly been repudiated." And he added: "I showed my recognition of the new situation by no longer calling my method of investigation and treatment *catharsis* but *psychoanalysis.*"[4] Enlightenment figure and part positivist that he was, Freud tended to equate analysis with reason itself.

Erikson, perhaps more than any other contemporary psychoanalyst, has been keenly aware of the dangers involved in literalizing Freudian method. That awareness has led him to be selective concerning his participation in what has been broadly called "the Americanization of psychoanalysis." Erikson has joined in with and contributed considerably to such pragmatic modifications of the procedure as altered frequency of visits (usually reductions from the original six per week), extensive use of face-to-face interviews, and a certain blending of psychoanalysis and psychotherapy. He has, however, been critical of American-induced technicization of the psychoanalytic procedure. Erikson has often recalled to colleagues and students the freer conversational style of Freud and his original followers in their psychoanalytic work as opposed to the more literal interpretation by scientific-minded American disciples of Freud's principle of the "neutral screen."

In addition, Erikson has, somewhat silently, evolved an extremely important principle of method that follows directly upon his configurational approach: *taking the overall environment into one's field of observation.* He applied this principle in early research on play configurations of children, and on the disrupted life patterns of American Indian tribes.[5] Similarly, in his later psychobiography of Luther one notes his imaginative immersion into the "overall environment" of the fifteenth and sixteenth centuries. And in his study of Gandhi he combines retrospective immersion into pre-independence India with direct observations (mostly through interviews) made in post-Gandhian India.

Erikson has always seen the clinical psychoanalytic environment as a very special laboratory, uniquely valuable in producing certain kinds of data but never to be mistaken for the actual world in which a person lives. Erikson's re-dignification of the overall environment, his recognition of its significance for the inner life of individuals, has been central to his conceptual breakthroughs.

In continuing to be an "analyst" Erikson perpetuates the interpretive analytic principle. At the same time he extends the principle of reason, again in a twentieth-century spirit, so that it becomes more wholistic and less bound to doctrinal assumptions about cause and effect. His term "originology" expresses his aversion to reductionism, atomization and the neglect of actual experience in favor of assumed early cause.

In his characteristically inclusive way, then, Erikson is both analytic and configurational. His broad-ranging sensibility permits him to harmonize these two modes most of the time. Where there seems to be conflict between them, the configurational mode invariably sets the tone of the interpretation. Thus it is the configuration of Luther's emerging identity (at a particular point in his life cycle) that enables him to resolve struggles and reach a new dimension of conscience. And it is Gandhi's identity at a special moment in his life that permits him to forge his method of nonviolence. Yet toward the end of each of these studies, Erikson restates analytic principles (around instinctual elements from early life) within the configuration, as if to insist that they can indeed be assimilated to it.

My own method also emerges from the Americanization of psychoanalysis. But in my use of depth-psychological research interviews, I have had to modify considerably the approaches I was taught during my clinical training. The method I have developed includes a greater stress on open dialogue and give-and-take within the interview (or, more rarely, group) situation. The exchanges rest upon a continuing dialectic between structure (careful formulation and checklist of areas to be probed) and spontaneity (encouragement of free association, dreams, and expression of feelings of any kind). Crucial to this method is the investigator's own psychological and moral confrontation with that which he investigates. That is, I have been aware of myself in all of my work as both an investigator who observes and as a person who acts upon, and is acted upon by, the other person or persons in the exchange and by the social environment in which the research is done.[6]

I have tried to locate the research interview, geographically and temporally, as closely as possible to the "psychohistorical interface" under study. To investigate Chinese thought reform, for instance, I interviewed Chinese and Westerners in Hong Kong as soon after their arrival from the mainland as I was able.[7] Similarly, my recent work with Vietnam veterans included "rap groups" and many forms of interviews and meetings, in most cases soon after their return from Vietnam and discharge from the military. The meetings were held sometimes at the veterans' own antiwar office, sometimes on "neutral ground" provided by a sympathetic religious group, and sometimes in my office at Yale or at a hotel where I was staying. In that work I entered into the veterans' struggles to renew themselves by means of examining their and society's participation in the war and evolving energizing principles beyond that participation. It could also be said that they entered into my struggles to renew myself through parallel examination of myself and my profession, even if we talked considerably less about my struggles than about theirs.[8]

In other work the principle has been similar, though applied to longer-range experience: in my interviews with Hiroshima survivors concerning the psychological impact of the atomic bomb conducted seventeen years after it had been dropped; in my work with Japanese youth in Tokyo and Kyoto from 1960 to 1962 (with preliminary work in 1958 and follow-up interviews in 1967) concerning their experience in culture change during the post–World War II years. In recent work there has been an especially close parallel between the issues being investigated in the research and the personal questions I pose for myself. In this work Eric Olson and I are interviewing innovative young men and women concerning struggles to be new kinds of professionals in ways that contribute to social change, and to consolidate in adult life some of the political and social critiques and cultural experiments of the late 1960s and early 1970s.

In general, the method embodies my efforts toward systematic observation, mostly at the individual level, of collective or shared forms of experience within a particular historical context. The method struggles toward a critical psychohistorical imagination in relationship to some of the most lethal aspects of twentieth-century life.

I have worked mostly in extreme historical situations, always assuming and seeking out connections between the extreme and the more ordinary. But for the paradigm I describe to take hold, I believe it will be necessary for the method to be extended to direct work with precisely such "ordinary" everyday experience and disturbance.

My own formative and interpretive mode carries Erikson's principle of configuration still further. I interpret individual feelings and actions on the basis of immediate struggles to harmonize and recast the forms and images that have been evolving over the course of the life cycle. That interpretation must include the emotional urgency of the process: the equation of threat to form with threat to life. One must consider the intensity with which form and meaning are defended, but also the capacity to survive precisely such threats (actual or metaphorical death immersions) and to re-create and even revitalize the forms of self and world.

From this standpoint, conflict occurring outside of awareness tends to involve competing forms, images, and acts. I have already suggested applications of this approach to my work with Hiroshima survivors and Vietnam veterans. I would add now that within the formative perspective, ethical struggles need not be viewed as reducible to something else (such as unconscious elements within the instinct-defense paradigm) or as outside of the interpretive system altogether. They can be seen as themselves integral to competing individual images and forms, and especially to the shared themes of the historical dimension. Much of the theoretical work bridging individual-psychological, ethical, and collective perspectives remains to be done. But this approach at least suggests that such bridges can be constructed—or perhaps not so much bridges as shared habitations.

Dreams, Symbols, and Imagination

Freud taught us that dreams are the *via regna* to the unconscious, and the greatness of his work on dreams lies in his elaborate and systematic demonstration of this truth. As is so often the case, however, the revolutionary breakthrough contained the seeds of its own narrow dogma. I have in mind Freud's conceptual insistence on "the wish," and its specific relationship to infantile psychosexual development, as the motivating principle of the dream. For Freud, the dream was an ingenius cover-up, a means by which unconscious ideas unacceptable to the conscious mind could find expression without becoming recognized for what they were. And the dream mechanisms—notably displacement and condensation—were in the service of this disguise, just as the overall dream process was in the service of permitting the dreamer to maintain his sleep.

Dream symbols had the same function: they were a representation—or substitution—of one idea or image for another, the two having been originally one. ("Things that are symbolically connected today were probably united in prehistoric times by conceptual and linguistic identity.") Such one-by-one symbolism, Freud thought, was "characteristic of unconscious ideation" in general. A particular symbol could, it was true, have "more than one or even several meanings," but there was always a "correct interpretation" that could be arrived at on the basis of the context and associations. So specific were these symbols—Emperor and Empress for the dreamer's parents, elongated objects for the male organ, rooms for women, etc.—that Freud raised the question of "whether many . . . do not occur with a permanently fixed meaning . . . like the 'grammalogues' in shorthand."[9]

Thus narrowly defined, the use of symbols became merely another dream mechanism to disguise infantile psychosexual meaning, all in the service of the dreamer's particular wish. All this had the effect of relegating Freudian dream theory to a self-enclosed interpretive chamber. And although Freud valued nothing more highly than the human imagination, his conceptual emphases tended to reduce the imaginative elements in dreams, as well as in other forms of mental activity, to the pejorative realm of pathological fantasy.

In the area of dream analysis, Erikson performed the perfect exercise for illustrating his method of inclusive extension of the classical psychoanalytic approach. He reexamined Freud's own celebrated "Irma dream"—that dream of all dreams—the first reported in *The Interpretation of Dreams*, and the dream Freud had in mind in his half-whimsical musing (in a letter to Fliess) about a possible tablet that might someday adorn his summer home carrying this inscription: "In this house, on July 24, 1895, the mystery of the dream unveiled itself to Dr. Sigm. Freud." In studying the Irma dream, Erikson carried out what I believe to be the most systematic application of his overall configurational approach, and in the process did much to reinvigorate psychoanalytic dream analysis. Erikson laid out an elaborate grid that included systematic exploration of not only the latent content of dreams (which Freud mostly concentrated upon) but the manifest content and the links between the two. And in an equally elaborate system of general reconstruction, he extended Freud's Irma dream both inwardly (to infantile psychosexual conflicts, which Freud hinted at but preferred at that point, for reasons of privacy, not to pursue) and outwardly (toward social process and collective identity). Finally, the entire reconstruction is subsumed to the overall paradigm of identity and the life cycle.

As Erikson spins his delicate web through interpersonal, affective, spatial, and temporal dimensions, he bears witness not only to Freud's formidable individual struggles around identity and generativity but to the significance of dreams in general, and of that dream in particular, for the discovery of psychoanalysis.[10] Here and elsewhere Erikson reasserts, for dreamers and dream analysts alike, the dignity and power of the imagination.

The paper does not escape a certain strain over its very inclusiveness. While admirably retrieving what he calls the vanishing art and ritual of exhaustive dream analysis, Erikson seems loath to leave out any conceivable aspect of either the instinctual or configurational paradigm. Yet he does neglect one area, that of death imagery and survivor guilt, to an even greater extent than did Freud (whose associations to his own dream suggested its great importance even if he did not grant it conceptual recognition). Still, in this relatively early essay of Erikson (first presented as a talk in 1949, though not published until 1954) we can find exciting intimations of a science of psychic forms.

My own sense of continuity with Freud and Erikson in the area of dream interpretation is suggested by a significant quotation from Freud which Erikson stresses: "The dream is fundamentally nothing more than a special *form* [Freud's emphasis] of our thinking, which is made possible by the conditions of the sleeping state. It is the dream-work which produces this form, and it alone is the essence of dreaming— the only explanation of its singularity."[11] With dreams, then, I would say, we are dealing with a special case within the mind's overall formative process.

But some of the "singularity" Freud mentions has to do with the extraordinary psychobiological power dreams may possess. For example, dreams can quite readily produce orgasm by means of sexual imagery alone[12] (in contrast, say, to pornographic films, which are very unlikely to result in anything more than sexual arousal). This impressive characteristic has never been satisfactorily explained. What it suggests, in addition to the dream's biological rootedness, is the force of its symbolized emotion. When one considers that force, together with the ingenious complexity dream symbolizations may also possess, we can begin to view the dream less as a "cover-up" and more as an "advanced" psychic domain that is both close to organicity and unique in imaginative reach. Dreams permit ephemeral experimentation with the freest play of images and the most radically absurd and innovative symbolizations.

In that sense, I have come to see dreams as notably prospective. Rather than being reducible to a particular wish or to infantile psychosexual struggles, dreams possess an exquisite immediacy in their creative rendition of "the state of the mind"—its conflicts and prospects. This does not mean that dreams cannot reflect the individual past or, for that matter, the collective past. In earlier work with Japanese youth, in fact, I tried to demonstrate the "historical dream."[13] The confusion arises over the false dichotomy between past and present or past and future. The "pastness" in a dream, the old elements from memory, can contribute in sophisticated ways to its experiential and prospective push toward new combinations and (in some cases) resolutions. Indeed that very "pastness," as a reservoir of formative suggestions and possibilities, can provide much of the energy for precisely these new combinations and resolutions.

The "dream work," or dream process, is the essence of the matter (as Freud said), and it can (as Erikson demonstrated) extend in virtually all directions. But rather than being limited to the two fundamental mechanisms of condensation and displacement, that dream work would seem to be nothing less than the anxious edge of the mind's explorations. Its ingenious symbolizations are highly subversive to the psychological status quo. This is so because of the sensitivity of the dream process to the contradictions and vulnerabilities of existing psychic forms, which is what we mean when we say that dreams reveal inner conflicts. It is the reason why dreams are so disturbing.

This combination of advanced symbolization and subversive impulse must have a great deal to do with dreams being relegated to sleep rather than waking life, as well as to our limited capacity for remembering them. But I think we should resist the temptation to dismiss all this as "repression," and instead consider some of the complexities here of cause and effect. The forgetting of dreams, considered from the standpoint of formative process, has to do with the blockage of psychic action, with desensitization or numbing. The unacceptability of their content undoubtedly has much to do with this blockage, as Freud suggested. But what might be most fundamentally at stake is the absence of forms and images that could relate to (and render significant, especially in a verbal way) the dream's "radical" view of psychic reality. Or, to say the same thing another way, the subversive formative suggestions of the dream can best take hold in the mind only if they can connect with relatively compatible elements within the more established "conservative" (even "reactionary") forms and "liberal compromise" that make up the conscious mind. Only then can dreams be remembered and contribute to prospective activity. Susanne Langer thus relates the dream to what she calls "incipient responses," meaning responses "which cannot possibly be all overtly carried out."[14] Involved in the forgetting of dreams is the subsuming of their psychic processes to the greater priority of a rival psychic "act" (set of processes with some culmination). Her emphasis upon "composition" parallels Erikson's on configuration, and she places great stress, as do many contemporary psychological investigators, upon the evolutionary importance of dreams for human image-making, for the imagination.[15]

We can thus view dreams as providing a perpetual dialectic between the most "primitive" psychic fragments and the most "enlightened" frontier of formative imagination. Within that dialogue the dream flashes its powerful and yet fluid symbolizations before us, ours for the using according to the mind's readiness and capacity. We can begin to appreciate the significance of this function by simply considering the dimensions of human image-hunger, our need for continuous psychic action, for combining and transforming every variety of mental element in our struggle for a waking sense of vitality. Crucial to this view of dreams, and to the formative process in general, is the distinction suggested in Chapter 2 between symbolism in the Freudian sense (the substitution of one thing for another, with a stress on specific sexual symbols) and a more broad and contemporary view of symbolization as the process of inner re-creation of *all* perception that characterizes human mental life.* This broader view does not exclude relatively consistent meanings for certain symbols, but holds open the ever present possibility that those meanings will be in turn joined or replaced by others in the continuous action of the formative process.

The dream thus teaches us a great deal about differing imaginative modes. In my work I have begun to make distinctions between relatively unconnected imagery and what I call "grounded imagination." Especially strong in the innovator, grounded imagination has roots in a person's living forms; and these roots permit a certain amount of freedom in imagining outward, so to speak, toward new (or new combinations of) images and original forms. The assumption here is that no form can be entirely new but must have imaginative grounding in older ones. Such grounding pro-

* "Dream components mean exactly whatever the dreamer wants to express by them, and that has to be found out by free association . . . ," is Guntrip's way of making a similar point.[16]

vides a suppleness in both centering and decentering—an agile "moving and bending" of images and ideas within a self that continues to cohere—that the innovator requires and at moments achieves. In contrast, the "normal" person (or the person with the numbing of normality) is reluctant to "imagine outward" very far from his familiar forms and remains intent upon returning to them very quickly when he does. Or else he or she may "let go" rather abruptly, with the resulting imagery having little viable connection with existing forms or possibility for contributing to new ones. With the psychotic, images are notably *ungrounded*, and neither they nor the forms to which they are tenuously related can cohere. Eric Olson and I have begun to observe the interplay of dream images, waking imagination, and form-making in a collage task we have been exploring. We find that "dream work," functioning as it does on so many levels, offers a particularly valuable area for the study of grounded and ungrounded imagination.

One way of approaching these issues is a simple exercise in which Olson and I and a number of our research subjects have now participated.[17] It consists of focusing, during the moments just before sleep, upon an immediate life struggle bound up with personal conflict and then "willing" a dream that will address that struggle. In the case of research subjects the images to be focused upon connect with a dominant theme of an interview being completed. We have found that one can "will" a dream in that manner and remember at least a portion of it in almost every case. The dreams themselves, of course, vary enormously. But through their associations we have consistently encountered strongly prospective patterns. The dream images, though they are usually quite removed in content from the dreamer's concept of his or her impasse, may nonetheless lead by way of associations toward altered

perspectives, forms beyond the impasse, and in some cases
directions of resolution.

Approach to History

Concerning the historical (or psychohistorical) dimension, I
have elsewhere discussed the sequence from Freud to Erikson to my own work.[18] Freud's strong inclination was to see
history as the individual psyche writ large. The principle of
"the return of the repressed," derived from individual psychology, was so central to Freud's understanding of the human collectivity that in his writings history becomes little but
repetition compulsion, and there is, psychologically speaking,
nothing new under the sun. Freud also held to a belief in historical transmission via the inheritance of primordial images,
a Lamarckian view that comes close to an organic mysticism.
This position was troubling even to Freud's immediate psychoanalytic disciples. It was, of course, also held by Jung.

The most significant of this primordial imagery, Freud be-
lieved, was that derived from the Darwinian principle of the
prehistorical primal horde. Freud thought this conception derived from a real event or series of events. The prehistorical
sequence involved a rebellion of sons against the father out
of sexual rivalry for the mother, and the sons' murder and
devouring of the father, the whole process creating the proto-
type of the Oedipus complex. Every human encounter between father and son as well as between ruler and ruled
becomes a replay of that primal event. And history itself—
including the creation of both religion and society in general
—becomes the working out and reworking of that perennially
inherited imagery of rebellion, murder, "oral incorporation,"
and guilt.[19]

Freud had a second model for historical interpretation, a

mode of interpretation drawn more directly from his clinical observations. This second model is exemplified by the Freud-Bullitt study of Woodrow Wilson, in which Wilson's struggles around masculinity become the explanation for his behavior at Versailles and for much of the post-Versailles world tragedy.[20]

Freud did have other views of history. At times he saw the human collectivity as capable of something close to progress through the renunciation of instinctual gratification in such achievements as the creation of monotheism, and in the gradual evolutionary development of man's more rational capacities, as contained in the ego. But the two basic models mentioned earlier were the ones he brought to the actual historical questions he addressed. The models do illuminate a great deal about the malignant repetition of historical themes. But in Freud's work and particularly in that of his followers they provide an all too ready basis for eliminating history in the name of studying it by collapsing history into the individual psyche.

Concerning issues of opposition, stability, and change, one must not underestimate the depth of Freud's own heresy. He boldly condemned and exposed conventional cultural hypocrisies. He struggled personally against those prevailing in the elite circles of the medical-scientific world within which he had been professionally formed and recognized as a brilliant and promising neurological researcher and practitioner. When excluded from a university career because of being Jewish, he called upon his Jewish identity as a source of extraordinary capacity to remain in opposition to prevailing groups and assumptions. But while Freud's theories shocked his contemporaries and troubled the sleep of much of Western civilization, those theories are statements of what Freud took to be relatively unchanging universal psychological forces. The psychological revolutionary, that is, put forth a profoundly conservative theory of human nature. Freud's view of history, moreover, was so dependent upon that concept of human nature that collective change or progress became either illusion or just one more manifestation of the same old thing—the rebellion of the primal horde—a return to the past under the visionary cloak of the future.[21] This view of history, together with his patriarchical character and his sense of conducting value-free scientific work, tended to place Freud in many situations on the side of "the father," of prevailing authority.

Inevitably he applied his Oedipal theory to disputes with his psychoanalytic disciples or to expressions among them of strong autonomy. I believe, however, that he was less antagonistic to intellectual disagreement *per se* than to the kind of originality (such as that of Jung and, in a very different way, that of Tausk) that he perceived as threatening to (or interfering with) his own evolving creative opus.[22]

To be sure, another side of Freud (great man that he was, he abounded in contradictions) did indeed note the existence of hard-won historical achievement, as in the example already cited of Moses bringing his version of monotheism to Jews (even if, as Freud argues in *Moses and Monotheism*, Moses was killed for his trouble in a reenactment of the primal murder, and was an Egyptian to boot). And in *Civilization and Its Discontents*, the most profound of Freud's later speculative volumes, Freud raises at least the possibility of the historical conquest of human self-destructiveness by means of collective revitalization of the life instincts, of Eros.[23] Most basically, though, Freud's outlook—one might say his cosmology—was grounded in the psychologically eternal. He held to a profoundly skeptical determinism that granted little possibility for significant change in individual or collective experience, because he viewed that experience as permanently shaped by individual and historical infancy.

Erikson takes a brilliant leap out onto the historical stage by immersing his imagination and that of his readers in the events of a particular epoch. Then, through his model of the great man (or woman) *in* history, he charts the ways in which that figure, in struggling toward a solution for overwhelming personal dilemmas, does the same for a significant collectivity and thereby initiates a breakthrough in human consciousness. In his already classic psychobiographies of Luther and Gandhi, Erikson employs Freudian principles molded into an identity configuration, but pays special attention to the all-important interface of individual and collective identities.[24]

In contrast to Freud, Erikson has been concerned throughout his work with the complexities of individual and social change. In fact, a major goal in Erikson's evolution of identity theory was to enable psychoanalytic ego psychology (within which he places his work) to address these complexities by means of a more responsive relationship to the social environment. But just as identity theory stresses individual continuity and sameness, so does Erikson stress his own continuity with the Freudian psychoanalytic movement and his reluctance to be in opposition to it. Long a controversial figure within psychoanalysis, he has often seemed to have much more in common with neo-Freudians than with his fellow Freudians, who have sometimes honored him, sometimes attacked him (as "sociological" or the like), and sometimes ignored him. But he has taught and supervised candidates in several Freudian institutes, and has maintained at least formal affiliation with classical psychoanalysis even when his main intellectual involvements have been elsewhere.

Erikson has now and then chided his colleagues, usually quite gently, for such things as their "originology" (exaggerated preoccupation with earliest infantile causation, as mentioned earlier) or for their potential suppression of creativity in "increasingly standardized and supervised" systems of psychoanalytic training.[25] But, having come to psychoanalysis as an "outsider" with minimal medical-scientific credentials, at a time when that beleaguered movement still existed mainly around Freud himself and was struggling with its own definitions of authority, Erikson has chosen not to engage in confrontations with that authority. As a way of being true to his own history, he has preferred instead to maintain a uniquely creative ambivalence to it. Reading his work in detail, one is impressed with the intellectual tightrope he has had to walk. But one is also impressed with the extent to which his achievement, while by no means solving all the questions debated by Freudians and neo-Freudians, renders most of those battles less significant than they seemed.

My own stress on "shared themes" has entailed working with groups of people who undergo an experience in common at some "psychohistorical interface" and who in some way can be demonstrated to affect, and be affected by, the historical process. I bring my formative perspective to the interviews themselves and also to whatever additional observations I can make on cultural and historical forces of importance in understanding the environments and the pasts of those whom I interview. I view all collective behavior as containing simultaneously three dimensions that we all too often artificially isolate: first, universal psychobiological elements, such as the nurturing needs of infants and children, and the inevitable problem of coping with death and dying;

second, cultural emphases and patternings, such as the Japanese stress on mother–child dependency and Japanese survivors' emphasis on continuing attachment to dead family members, as opposed to American stress upon separation and autonomy in both of these situations; and, finally, recent or contemporary historical forces—the kinds of psychohistorical dislocation we have discussed, including those around nurturing and death, or, more specifically, the Chinese Communist replacement of Confucian stress on moderation and restraint with expressions of near-Dionysian revolutionary enthusiasm.

The work moves from the empirical (direct interview data, usually recorded) to the comparative (observations on similarities and differences between the group being studied and other relevant groups) to the more speculative dimension of the significance of these shared themes and comparative principles for the overall historical era. In seeking concepts that connect the individual with history, I have been concerned with issues having to do with time and change; with modes of transformation, restoration, and accommodation that are applicable both to the person and to the collectivity; as well as with the "Protean" or experimental psychological style already mentioned. These bridging concepts make great demands upon language. In my judgment the creation of a more systematic psychohistory awaits the elaboration of a more extensive vocabulary to depict connecting patterns and forms.[26]

I too have a dialectic of continuity and heresy in relationship to what may broadly be called psychoanalytic authority. While much farther, generationally and in other ways, from psychoanalytic origins than Erikson, both Freudian and neo-Freudian psychoanalysis have had great importance to my intellectual formation and continue to matter to me now.

Despite early doubts about much of what I saw to be psychoanalytic dogma, I originally intended to become a psychoanalyst, as did most enterprising psychiatric residents at that
time. I was quite confused by the experience of first being
rejected by two psychoanalytic institutes (who seemed to
associate my outspoken tendencies with "instability") and
then a bit later being accepted by two more. I chose the Boston Psychoanalytic Institute, despite its reputation for extreme orthodoxy (quite justified, I am afraid, at least then).
I did so because I had important intellectual affiliations at
Harvard and in the Cambridge-Boston area. I had completed
my study of Chinese thought reform and had been awarded a
long-term research grant for further "research and research
training" around my interests of individual psychology and
historical change, particularly in East Asia. I was determined
to grope idiosyncratically toward whatever it was I would become, rather than building my life around a particular psychoanalytic institute. Moreover, despite the greater intellectual orthodoxy in Boston the human atmosphere there struck
me as less authoritarian than at the other ostensibly more
"liberal" institute that had accepted me. It is also quite possible that something in me wanted to grapple with psychoanalysis as close as possible to its ideological source.

But what lent something close to a quality of absurdity to
the enterprise was that, during my two years at the institute,
I was completing my book on Chinese thought reform, in the
last section of which I raised questions about psychoanalytic
training in relationship to criteria for ideological totalism
established earlier in the study. I was concerned about the
extent to which the trainee's combined roles of patient, student, and candidate can cause the atmosphere in the institute
to approach "milieu control," "a near-mystical aura," and "an
implicit demand for ideological purity"—a "confession proc-

ess" that calls forth "neurotic and existential guilt" in undermining criticism, tendencies toward "loading of the language," the suggestion of a "sacred science," the "primacy of
doctrine over person," and "the dispensing of [psychoana-
lytic] existence."[27] My tone was measured, but the subject
was, to say the least, touchy for everyone. My having formed
those questions on the basis of my research and personal experience gave me a rather special stance, one of critical re-
serve, as a psychoanalytic candidate.

During my two-year association with the institute I had
the impression that my concerns were not without foundation and that there was indeed a prevailing core of totalism.
My psychoanalytic teachers were considerate and responsive to my idiosyncratic requests: I was granted a two-year
leave of absence, for instance, for previously planned research
in Japan. My personal analysis with Beata Rank provided
considerable help to me in connection with various psychological struggles but was neither philosophically exciting nor
a fundamental turning point in my life. The seminars at the
institute, although on the whole narrowly gauged and unin-
spiring, had and continue to have considerable value for me
in deepening my intellectual encounter with the classical
psychoanalytic paradigm.

Upon returning from Japan two years later to begin my
appointment at Yale, I decided to discontinue my psychoanalytic training. That decision had to do with continuing
and perhaps deepening ideological differences and with an
increasing sense of myself as a particular kind of research
psychiatrist who had no great need to become a psychoanalyst. What I did not realize at the time was that through this
severing of my institutional connection with psychoanalysis
my intellectual roots in it could be strengthened and made
more pliable. It was only slightly with tongue in cheek that I

once wrote: "To reevaluate—and rediscover—Freudianism and Freud via Chinese thought reform and Mao Tse-tung respectively may sound a bit strange, but that is the way it has been for me."[28]

Over the years I have expressed myself more often than has Erikson in specific opposition to a number of Freud's concepts, such as his approaches to history, to the psychology of women, and to the conceptualization of death and guilt. Yet I have always been aware of benefiting greatly from taking seriously Freud's way of exploring problems like these. The whole issue of guilt, for example, has become increasingly central to my work on psychological change and historical transformation.[29] Freud's position emphasizes the archaic quality of guilt, its evolution from remnants of childhood if not prehistoric memory; and the harsh, condemning, judgmental character and inertial quality that sets guilt in opposition to insight, change, and health. My experience, first in studying thought reform and later in interviewing atomic-bomb and Vietnam War survivors, has led me to distinguish between static and potentially animating forms of guilt. Static forms of guilt may include a great deal of numbing and resistance to feeling or, in contrast, may have a self-punitive, self-lacerating *mea culpa* quality. Animating guilt, on the other hand, always connects with an image beyond the guilt and moves toward change. In this sense animating guilt is the anxiety of responsibility and is a vital emotion for individual and species survival. As we distance ourselves from the experience of guilt through technology, large bureaucratic structures, and political language which sustains numbing, we decrease our capacity for feeling and for assuming responsibility for our individual and collective destinies. In my study on thought reform and again in my book on antiwar Vietnam veterans, I described a pattern of psychological change involving confrontation, reordering of images and forms, and renewal of self and world. Animating guilt is vital for energizing such a process.[30]

My oppositional views on issues of psychological theory are related to concerns with holocaust and transformation in general and with psychological change in particular. I have already mentioned my frequent finding that a state of "harmony" or "stability," rather than being antagonistic to change (or struggle toward change), may in fact require it. Similarly, psychic survival frequently depends upon the creation and re-creation of images and forms that can combine fluidity with sufficient symbolic power to touch what I have called the "mythic" or "formative zone" of the psyche. We require models for opposition and change over the generations that are more dialectical and subtle than Freud's image of patricide. By taking a fresh look at currents of authority and opposition in mentorship and discipleship, teaching and learning, and parent–child relations, the new model could allow for extensive give-and-take that includes mutual playfulness and flexibility, with moments of seeming reversal of roles. There can be the expectation that the disciple will not become a carbon copy of the mentor but will draw upon the latter's imaginative qualities and "life story," as experienced in their relationship, in shaping whatever combination of continuity and transformation he or she brings to that which has been learned.[31]

Psychoanalysis (and "psychoformation" too) is subject to the vicissitudes of death and renewal as experienced over generations of mentorship and discipleship. And there is no telling whether psychoanalysis will be revitalized (as Erikson believes and works toward) or whether it will instead give way to a body of thought that both draws upon it and takes its own new shape, as the subtitle of this volume suggests.

CHAPTER 5

Survivor as Creator

In groping toward an understanding of the survivor's struggle for form one turns naturally to the experience of the artist, and to what I shall broadly term the literature of survival. The artist is a prophet of forms. And when forms are in radical disarray, the artist suggests patterns of reordering, even if, in the process, seeming to contribute further to the disarray. For it is the artist's task, one that is insufficiently noted, to reveal to us the exquisite details of the experience of desymbolization. An examination of the literature of survival can contribute to an understanding of the overall problem of formulation.

"We are survivors in this age," Herzog writes in one of his unsent letters, "so theories of progress ill become us . . . To realize that you are a survivor is a shock. At the realization of such election you feel like bursting into tears." Herzog goes on to suggest that from history's endless succession of wars, revolutions, and famines "perhaps we, modern mankind (can it be!), have done the nearly impossible, namely, learned something."[1]

Exactly what mankind—and Herzog—may have learned remains ambiguous. But whatever it is the survivor "knows," that knowledge is bound up with the dialectic between life and death, with "dying" and being "reborn." In my Hiroshima

113

study I defined the survivor as "one who has come into contact with death in some bodily or psychic fashion and has himself remained alive."[2] I spoke of a survivor ethos, thrust into special prominence by the holocausts of the twentieth century, imposing upon all of us a series of immersions into death which mark our existence. I would go further now and say that we are survivors not only of holocausts which have already occurred but of those we imagine or anticipate as well.

Five psychological patterns characterize the survivor. The first has to do with the survivor's indelible death image and death anxiety. This "death imprint" often includes a loss of a sense of invulnerability. The second pattern, that of death guilt, is revealed in the survivor's classic question, "Why did I stay alive when he or she or they died?" The question itself stems from a sense of organic social balance: "If I had died, he or she would have lived." That image of exchange of one life for another is perhaps the survivor's greatest psychological burden. A third pattern is that of desensitization, diminished capacity to feel, or what I call psychic numbing—the breakdown of symbolic connectedness with one's environment. Numbing is a necessary protective mechanism in holocaust, but can become self-perpetuating and express itself in sustained depression, despair, and apathy or withdrawal. A fourth pattern derives from the "death taint" associated with a "morbid contamination." The result includes mutual suspicion and distrust which survivors often experience toward each other, and social discrimination to which they are subjected in relation to others. Basic to this pattern is the survivor's "suspicion of counterfeit nurturance"—the combination of feeling in need of help while resenting that help which is offered, since it confirms an inner sense of weakness. The survivor's bitterness arises from these antagonistic feelings.

The fifth pattern is fundamental to all survivor psychology, and encompasses the other four. This is the struggle toward inner form or formulation, the quest for significance in one's death encounter and remaining life experience. This formulative struggle is equally visible in more symbolic experiences of holocaust, those of surviving ways of life that one perceives to be "dying." In that sense, not only holocaust but rapid social change makes survivors of us all.

Participation in holocaust renders the survivor vulnerable to deformations, dislocations and imaginative impediments. The hard-won "knowledge" of death that both defines and plagues the experience of survival tends to be fragmentary at best and half articulate. Yet that knowledge is precious in the extreme. It takes shape from the struggle to grasp the death encounter and render it significant. Only by coming to such knowledge can the survivor cease to be immobilized by the death imprint, death guilt, and psychic numbing. That is, in struggling to reorder his or her own experience, the survivor can contribute to the general historical reordering so widely craved. And these psychological emanations—from past holocausts and their survivors, from anticipated holocausts and their imagined survivors—reach everyone. The painful wisdom of the survivor can, at least potentially, become universal wisdom.

What I am suggesting is that to "touch death" and then rejoin the living can be a source of insight and power. This is true not only for those exposed to holocaust, or to the death of a parent or lover or friend, but also for those who have permitted themselves to experience fully the "end of an era," personal or historical.

Albert Camus: The Gentle Survivor

We could draw upon any of the arts; but a philosophical artist such as Albert Camus is especially revealing because he tells us what he is doing as he does it. While this approach can at moments subvert the subterranean source of the art, it has its own special historical value. When we look back at Camus and compare him with some of his literary successors, he seems a relatively gentle kind of World War II survivor. His Nobel Prize acceptance speech of 1957 is, among other things, a proclamation of a literature of survival that had already existed through, in Camus' phrase, "twenty years of absolutely insane history."[3]

Camus saw as the "task" of his generation—or what we could call its survivor mission—that of "keeping the world from destroying itself." But much of the force of this public vision derived from very personal experiences in the underground during World War II, as epitomized by the death of his comrade-in-arms, fellow writer and close friend, René Leynaud. As Camus later wrote, "In thirty years of life no death reverberated within me like this one."[4] He also spoke of "paltry excuses of those who remain alive." And throughout his work he wrote of his own "temptation of hatred [which] had to be overcome"; of his sense of loss ("that strength of love which has been taken from us forever"); and of his and his generation's struggle to construct "an art of living in times of catastrophe in order to be reborn by fighting openly against the death instinct at work in our history."

Camus' stand on survival emerged from this particular way of applying his imagination—as evolved through his individual-psychological experience—to the holocausts of his time. When he asked rhetorically, "Do you know that over a period of twenty-five years, between 1922 and 1947, seventy million Europeans—men, women, and children—have been uprooted, deported, and killed?" his question arose from his own organic knowledge of that history. He insisted (as his leading biographer, Germaine Brée, tells us) upon viewing such things as "a scandal that he himself finds impossible to evade." The scandal includes not only these millions of deaths but the act of living on in the face of them. And though that scandal is diminished by ethical acts which render the deaths significant, and though Camus, as much as any writer, extolled life in his lyrical evocation of the Algerian sun and sea and its "invincible summer," he never lost his sense that there was something scandalous about having survived so much.

Caligula[5] is Camus' most vivid rendition of the absurd survivor, and one of the most important plays ever written about the aberrations of the survivor state. Formerly the epitome of the just ruler (living by the principle that "the only mistake one makes in life is to cause others suffering"), Caligula is suddenly transformed by the death of his sister, Drusilla. He had loved her, and with "more than brotherly feelings." But what overwhelms him is neither guilt nor loss *per se* but the realization that the world lacks order or meaning, that "men die and they are not happy," and that "men weep because the world's all wrong."

Caligula embarks upon a systematic course of victimization and murder, of rewarding evil and punishing good and a general perversion of all values by which he and his subjects formerly lived. We can understand his actions as illustrating Rilke's principle that "killing is one of the forms of our wandering mourning." What Caligula mourns beyond the loss of his sister is a lost bond with higher powers, a lost sense of immortality. He kills in order to achieve a new transcendence, convinced as he is that "there's only one way of getting even with the gods: all that's needed is to be as cruel as they." He wants what is unattainable—the omnipotence of *literal* immortality. He must continue to kill in order to perpetuate the illusion that he can obtain such immortality: "When I don't kill I feel alone." Hence his dying words, "I'm still alive!"

Camus explains Caligula's ways as being "unfaithful to mankind through fidelity to himself." This fidelity in rebellion against death and dislocation has in it a quest, however misdirected and pathological, to overcome the broken connection so intolerable to this kind of absurd survivor. Caligula is not redeemed; but by revealing the most extreme consequences of the unformulated survivor state—the passage from the absurd to the omnipotent survivor—he carries us toward insight.

In *The Stranger*[6] we recognize, in a single murder, a similar attempt to recover a sense of vitality. Meursault is incapable of mourning for his dead mother; he feels nothing, is totally numbed, cannot "shed a single tear." When shortly afterward in a somewhat murky altercation he shoots an anonymous Arab, we think again of the connection between impaired mourning and murderous violence. Meursault is brought to legal justice and condemned to death as much for his seeming inhumanity at his mother's funeral as for the crime itself.

In a dramatic scene with a priest in his death cell, Meursault angrily condemns the priest's clichés and unconvincing promises of immortality. In feeling himself, and imagining his mother to have felt, "on the brink of freedom, ready to start life all over again," Meursault realizes the absurd survivor's liberation in the face of death by means of what Camus called "lucidity." For Camus lucidity means not only clarity, consciousness, and truth, but (as suggested by its Latin roots) a state of being luminous, fused with light, and thereby transcending the rote and prosaic without recourse to false gods. Yet this lucidity and (in Camus' words) "the extra life it involves" depend "not on man's will, but on its contrary, which is death." The book ends with a ringing defiance of all ethical hypocrisy: "For all to be accomplished, for me to feel less lonely, all that remained to hope was that on the day of my execution there would be a huge crowd of spectators and that they should greet me with howls of execration." In that sentence the absurd survivor becomes an insurgent.

The insurgent survivor is epitomized by Camus' two most celebrated heroes, the rebel and the plague physician. Camus meant his rebel[7] or insurgent survivor to be more radical than even a conventional revolutionary because he is more fundamentally critical, subversive, and formative. There is no revolution to be, once and for all, achieved, there is permanence only in questioning and insurgency. The insurgent survivor rebels, to be sure, against injustice, murder and suffering, against victimization of any kind. But he also rebels, Camus tells us, against the core of human existence, the fact of death. His "rejection of death," however, is his "desire for immortality and for clarity." What he rejects, in other words, is meaningless or formless death; what he seeks through his rebellion is transcendence by means of ever renewed human forms. "If nothing lasts, then nothing is justified," he reasons, so that "to fight against death amounts to claiming that life has a meaning, to fighting for order and for unity."

At bottom, then, the insurgent survivor is a form-seeker and form-giver. His quest "to learn to live and to die, in order to be a man, to refuse to be a god," goes a step beyond absurdity into form. The insurgent seeks to reestablish a sense of immortality that is both biological and creative and to do so through "the movement of life" and "its purest outburst." Camus insists that "in the light the earth remains our first and last love," and that with living justice "our brothers are breathing under the same sky" so that "there is born that strange joy which helps one live and die, and which we shall never again renounce to a later time." He presents us a survivor mission to live in autonomous connection rather than surrender ourselves to a totalistic vision of the future. He is making a plea for an immortality that is symbolic and fluid rather than literal and fixed.

As a giver of forms the insurgent survivor must perforce become a healer. Dr. Rieux, the central figure of *The Plague*,[8] is called upon to provide both medical and spiritual therapy. His antagonist is not only the plague itself but the more general evil the plague stands for—"the feeling of suffocation from which we all suffered and the atmosphere of dread and exile in which we lived." But knowledge and memories—rejection of illusion, connection with the past, and lucidity toward the present and the future—count for much. And the survivor's special knowledge of death, and simple formulation of duty to life, provide rebellious courage and healing power.

The progression from first- to second-generation literature of survival is presaged in Camus' own shift (in such later works as *The Fall* and *The Renegade*) from compassionate insurgency to acerbic misanthropy. It is the progression from Camus' searching irony to the outlandish mockery of Kurt Vonnegut and Gunter Grass. Rather than bemoan human dislocation, this literature of mockery (a more accurate and comprehensive term, I believe, than "black humor") seizes that dislocation with ebullience and even joy. It extends the principle of gallows humor to society (or nonsociety) at large. Gallows humor mocks the death that awaits one and, in its combination of rebellion and laughter, at least suggests the existence of a more humane order. The literature of mockery views all of contemporary history—and perhaps mankind itself—as moribund if not already dead. Mockery then provides a kind of literary wake: a vigil or "watch" over the dead social body prior to burial. It offers a means of expressing anguish and of crying out against the cruelly haphazard gods of death and loss, but at the same time a form of liberation and release, and at least in some cases a celebration of life in the midst of death.

We gravitate naturally to the mocking and mocked anti-hero. Whether a mere figure of our impotence or a man thrust into greatness despite himself, he evokes not cosmic order (as a tragic hero does) but our cosmic disorder. In this literature death and madness are respected; what is savagely mocked is the "sanity" of everyday life which dissolves the significance both of death and of man's quest for immortality. The central point about mockery is that it *confronts* the phenomena involved, our situation and ourselves.

In our age of madness, Warren Miller tells us in his novel *Looking for the General,*[9] madness itself becomes not only an expectation but a "duty": "I mean that: duty—of the sane to pursue madness, to pursue, search, seek out, claim or beg for themselves a tiny portion of that manna, even the merest smudge of that magic dust, sweet pollen that clings to madness's bird-body, gilding feathers, touching breast's filmy down with its flowery gold powder." Madness is a duty, not only because of the unacceptability of what passes for sanity but because the mad state itself provides a form of transcendence. The literature of mockery seems to be telling us that the "manna" or "magic dust" of madness may represent the liberating core of our survivor wisdom. Inevitably the literature of mockery is ambivalent toward madness. William Carlos Williams' statement "The pure products of America go crazy" could be interpreted to mean "are driven crazy and destroyed" or "become crazy as the only path to wisdom." Or, to put the problem in the form of a question: If those we call "normal" are (according to wiser standards) really insane, does that mean that those we call "insane" are a source of knowledge and health?

Above all, madness becomes equated with a renaissance of fantasy and the rediscovery of the childlike wonder of play. There are German myths of the end or near-end of the world in which the only survivors are children who re-create the world through play. Children's play provides the imaginative forms that constitute the evolving mind, and the psychic sense of life. But over the course of "lived history" such play becomes a more grim business, suffused as it is with the sobering lessons of years of accompanying unplay. This unplay—with its mixture of injustice, unpleasantness and necessity—enters prominently into a formulation of self and world that must forevermore accompany whatever playfulness is retained. The mocking survivor has a mixed memory, and memory is the essence of the survivor as creator. Again Herzog: "But I, with my memory—all the dead and the mad are in my custody, and I am the nemesis of the would-be forgotten."

Kurt Vonnegut: Duty-Dance with Death

Kurt Vonnegut identifies himself directly as a survivor of holocaust and brings a special kind of bite to the literature of mockery. His two great external themes are Dresden and Hiroshima. His more general themes are man's death-dealing stupidities, and beyond those (as he puts it in his introduction to *Slaughterhouse Five*) "plain old death." "Dutydance," part of the sub-subtitle of *Slaughterhouse Five*, is an accurate description of Vonnegut's imaginative enterprise.

In *Mother Night*,[10] an earlier novel, Howard Cambell, as survivor of Nazism and much else, can only conclude, "All people are insane. They will do anything at any time, and God help anybody who looks for reasons." And in the same vein: "I've lost the knack of making sense. I speak gibberish to the civilized world, and it replies in kind." Here survivor wisdom lies in recognizing how impaired our post-holocaust formulations of the world really are, how lost we are in our "gibberish"—a message which, at least in Vonnegut's hands, becomes a powerful formulation of its own.

In *Cat's Cradle*[11] Vonnegut directs his "formative gibberish" to Hiroshima. The life-giving force in this book, its mocking formulation, is "Bokononism," a collection of "bittersweet lies" put together by a black adventurer who found himself cast adrift on and enchanted by the little Caribbean Isle of San Lorenzo. There he "cynically and playfully invented a new religion." In a Bokononist poem Vonnegut is specific about the principle of formative gibberish:

> Tiger got to hunt,
> Bird got to fly;
> Man got to sit and wonder, "Why, why, why?"
> Tiger got to sleep,
> Bird got to land;
> Man got to tell himself understand.

But we have to turn to Vonnegut's great survivor novel, *Slaughterhouse Five*,[12] for a sense of the exalted possibilities of mockery. *Slaughterhouse Five* is less about Dresden *per se* than it is about a state of mind evoked in Vonnegut by the destruction of Dresden. Vonnegut is therefore talking about war and holocaust, and about man's tendency to accelerate the arrival and demean the process of "plain old death." The novel is a survivor's effort to make sense—or antisense—of a world dominated by every variety of holocaust and every variety of numbing.

The key to the "telegraphic-schizophrenic"—that is, the condensed—mad style and content of this book is the recurrent phrase "So it goes." This is the Tralfamadorean shrug-commentary on all deaths, since the inhabitants of that planet believe that "when a person dies he only *appears* to die." Vonnegut uses the phrase all through the book with a combination of gaiety and terror, as a form of mocking witness to man's unfeeling murders, to his equally unfeeling survival of those murders, and to precisely the resignation that the phrase suggests. "So it goes," then, unifies the diverse film-like flashes that make up the book's sequence as Billy Pilgrim moves back and forth between his family and optometry office in Illium, New York, wartime Germany, various psychiatric hospitals, and the planet of Tralfamadore. Billy himself is a kind of death-guide for twentieth-century man.

Slaughterhouse Five is about feeling and not feeling, about remembering and not remembering, about looking and not looking back, about dying and not dying, about living and not living. Vonnegut is right there with Billy all through the book. He has Billy suggest, as "a good epitaph for Billy Pilgrim—and for me too, EVERYTHING WAS BEAUTIFUL AND NOTHING HURT." The little tombstone containing the epitaph is that of Billy, Vonnegut, Nixon, all of us—the tombstone of all who half-live in our present age of numbing.

Gunter Grass's Dwarf Drummer: The Realization of the Grotesque

It is hard to say how much Vonnegut's work has been influenced by Grass's early classic in the post–World War II literature of mockery, *The Tin Drum*,[13] but the two authors have a great deal spiritually in common. Instead of the clipped, bittersweet apocalypse in Vonnegut's work, Grass gives us an elaborately convoluted, one could even say epic, form of the mocking grotesque.

The story is told, or rather drummed out, by an inmate who considers his mental hospital bed "a goal attained at last . . . my consolation." He is, of course, none other than Oskar Matzerath, that dwarf drummer and literary original who, according to his stepmother (and first mistress), "don't know how to live and . . . don't know how to die." He is, however, a genius at surviving.

Oskar, again in the tradition of the literature of mockery, is both all-knowing and hopelessly regressive in his consuming urge to return to that hallowed place under the skirts of his potato-gathering grandmother. But his regression is always brilliantly in the service of subversion, so that on his third birthday he makes the fatal decision to grow no more. The key to Oskar's perennial survivals is his tin drum. The drum not only permits him to resist his impulse to scurry back to the womb, but is also his means of recording his own history and history in general. The drum is incorruptible and resists Oskar's attempts to forget segments of his own past. Its most fundamental purpose is social and ethical:

> For it is not only demonstrations of a brown hue that I attacked with my drumming. Oskar huddled under the rostrum for Reds and Blacks, for Boy Scouts and Spinach Shirts, for Jehova's Witnesses, the Kyffauser Bund, the Vegetarians and the young Polish Fresh Air Movement. Whatever they might have to sing, trumpet, or proclaim, my drum knew better.

The drum "knew better" because its own immortal vision transcends these ephemeral collectivities.

Grotesque form, visionary drum, and miraculous glass-shattering thus enable this diminutive mocking survivor to expose and outlast the absurd history that normal adults have created. Oskar's survivals include the most extreme manifestations not only of absurd evil but of man's hypocritical and conventional attraction to that evil.

Grass concretizes the survivor ethos in Oskar's witnessing

of individual deaths around him. Oskar's grandfather, his mother, and his mother's lover each die in ways that epitomize both the person and the epoch. Oskar's archetypal death encounter inevitably takes place with the demise of his father, Matzerath, who embodies all that Oskar despises but is himself caught up in. Matzerath dies by choking on his Nazi party badge. But Oskar concludes (with characteristic honesty) "that he [Oskar] had killed Matzerath deliberately," that Matzerath had choked both "on the Party" and "on me, his son" and that, in any case, he (Oskar) "was sick of dragging a father around with him all his life."

The themes of fatherlessness and father–son reversal are partly a reflection of dislocation and moral inversion, partly a call to liberation. Oskar's father's funeral is the occasion for a "decision" to start growing again, and although for Oskar this leads to a still greater deformation, we can see in the decision a rarely acknowledged side of the survivor ethos—the survivor's capacity to experience the death he has witnessed as a form of release and new beginning.

However undisinfectable life and death may be, whatever Oskar's apparent inability to mourn his losses or to find significance in the face of them, his gift of mockery keeps him oriented toward the living. But Oskar's ultimate strength lies in his infinite flexibility. Our little hero, attaining near the end of the book a mad-grotesque form of maturity, can contemplate his future with Protean exuberance: "Yet so many possibilities are open to a man of thirty."

The spiritual journey must include recurrent visits with terror and evil—with the Black Witch. For Protean (contemporary) man is pursued by terror and evil, by his own betrayals. He has no choice but to live in the memory and expectation of holocaust. But one can also know transcendence. For Oskar certain enduring objects and memories take on immortal qualities, including "the secret parts of a few women and young girls, my own pecker, the plastic watering can of the boy Jesus . . . , my drumsticks, from my third birthday on . . . , my umbilical cord, as I sat playing with it . . ." The journey is precarious, replete with disaster, but it is exuberant, open, and (here is the hope) endless.

Pornographic Confrontation

Grass's style of grotesquery takes us directly to still another, in a way ultimate, form of the literature of survival, the pornographic confrontation. Involved here is the use of underground images, publicly forbidden but close enough to virtually everyone's inner life to be privately (or semiprivately) shared.

When Geoffrey Gorer first spoke of "the pornography of death" he referred to the contemporary habit of offering fantasies of extreme violence to mass audiences. Gorer saw this pornography as more or less pathological, arising from our unhealthy repression of death imagery, just as ordinary (sexual) pornography on a large scale reflects widespread sexual repression. Gorer's view is the psychoanalytic one: repressed ideas never disappear but reemerge in harmful distorted form; therapy consists of uncovering that which has been repressed so that it can be dealt with in more conscious, rational ways. But if, as I believe, the problem is less repression of death than impairment in the general capacity to create viable forms around it, the pornography of death takes on a somewhat different function. It represents an exposé of our distorted views of death, an extreme rendition of our state of desymbolization. Pornography then becomes a means of revelation by excess. Through what Gabriel Marcel called the "provocative nudity of death" it provides a necessary insight into our condition that is indispensable to, and ultimately inseparable from, the new forms for which we hunger.

Much of Norman Mailer's work is directed at this kind of pornographic confrontation. What may appear to be wallowing in violence can in fact be a form of exploring the excessive—the pornographic—dimensions of death. *An American Dream*[14] is a novel with a special kind of concern with the death encounter, not at all grasped by most of its critics. The book is an account of a survivor's experiential journey following his wartime killing of four Germans, an act which showed him equal to the death encounter but which at the same time left him with a permanent death imprint—an awesome realization that "death was a creation more dangerous than life."

At moments Rojak, the central figure in the book, experiences a survivor's sense of having conquered death. But mostly he feels overwhelmed by death anxiety, by "a private kaleidoscope of death" that cannot be relieved by his theoretical insight (he is a teacher of existential psychology) that "magic, dread and the perception of death are the roots of all motivation." To still his anxiety he challenges and courts death, becomes preoccupied with suicide and murder. Rojak's act of murdering his wife is an effort to overcome his own fear of extinction, stave off suicide, reassert his mastery over death, achieve through killing a sense of transcendence, and absorb some of the immortal power of his wife's evil (later he has a fantasy of eating her flesh).

A key arena for pornographic confrontation is what is usually called the "theater of the absurd" but is better termed the Theater of the Dead. One could speak here of Genet and Ionesco, of earlier influences of Artaud and Brecht, and more recent developments of Grotowski and the Living Theater. But I think the key figure for our time is Samuel Beckett.

"The living are dead . . . and the dead live," a feeling expressed by Heinrich Böll's disintegrating artist-clown, could well sum up Beckett's world. It is a dead universe, or rather a universe in which life has become so numbed as to be more dead than death.

One could draw upon **any** number of Beckett people from his plays or stories or musings, but he is most explicit in his play *Krapp's Last Tape*.[15] More than just an incongruous and pathetically humorous figure, Krapp is a man neither dead nor alive. What characterizes his existence is constant self-survival *and no more*.

The sixty-nine-year-old Krapp can live only through one old tape recording to which he continually returns, seeking out that moment of love described on it. But the thirty-nine-year-old Krapp on that tape had come to the same conclusion—the refrain of a lost youth, meaningless life, expressed throughout the play, along with a denial that he would have it otherwise. The play ends with Krapp staring motionlessly before him and the tape running on "in silence." Beckett's pornographic confrontation is that of a special twentieth-century form of death in life, a form of total numbing in which mechanical recordings, echoing a series of survivals, replace the act of living.

There is a common theme running through Camus' gentility, Grass's grotesquery, Vonnegut's death dance, Borowski's unspeakable ironies (in *This Way for the Gas, Ladies and Gentlemen*), Dr. Strangelove's nuclear insanity and Beckett's death in life. They all tell us that civilization—human life itself—is threatened, dying or dead; that we must recognize this death or near-death, pursue it, record it, and enter into it if we are to learn the truth about ourselves, if we are to live. This capacity for intimacy with (and knowledge of) death in the cause of renewed life is the survivor's special quality of imagination, his special wisdom. But how can that wisdom be shared? Can survivors be mentors to the world?

In connection with my Hiroshima work, for instance, I have been asked such questions as: How can you be at all certain that it will be useful? Couldn't it bring about further numbing? Or, worse, encourage a large-scale shelter program in order to be properly prepared for nuclear war? Or, simply, so what?

My answer has to do with human capacity to bring imagination to bear upon unpalatable existential-historical truths, to expand the limits of that imagination on behalf of species survival. If one is to overcome psychic numbing one must break out from the illusions supporting that numbing and begin, in Martin Buber's words, "to imagine the real." One must learn to do what has heretofore not been possible for us, to imagine nuclear disaster—that is, to imagine the "end of the world."

Hiroshima's relationship to the rest of us, then, has mainly to do with the imagination. The gap between technology and imagination remains a formidable one, as evident in the relative poverty of general creative response. Alain Resnais' film *Hiroshima Mon Amour,* the novel *Black Rain* by Masuji Ibuse, the images conveyed by John Hersey in his pioneering journalistic pilgrimage, and my own psychological study have all been in the service of narrowing the imaginative gap.

End-of-the-World Imagery

One gains a vivid sense of the importance of end-of-the-world imagery from the description by the nuclear physicist Eugene Rabinowitch. He writes of his "vision of crashing skyscrapers under a flaming sky" while walking through the streets of Chicago during the hot 1945 summer, and of his subsequent sleeplessness and renewed dedication in redrafting what was to become the "Franck Report" opposing the dropping of the atomic bomb without warning on a populated city.[16] Involved here is an anticipatory imagination capable of sensitivity to a trend of events which other people have become numbed to. I know from conversations with many such people that they have strong inclinations—inclinations which can be described as at the border of talent and neurosis—toward imagining, seeing before themselves, various kinds of holocaust and disaster.

In *Death in Life* I wrote of the quest of the despot to become an "eternal survivor," a quest which can lead to virtually everyone else becoming a corpse. The necessity for, and the precariousness of, end-of-the-world imagery creates a dilemma which is reflected in the life of Dag Hammarskjold, Secretary General of the United Nations from 1953 until he was killed in a plane crash in September 1961. Hammarskjold constantly warned against nuclear war and succeeded in conveying to the world some of the constructive force of the apocalyptic imagery so strong within him. It was not until the publication of his diary, *Markings*,[17] that the personal meaning of some of this imagery for him could begin to be understood. Describing a perpetual struggle for self-realization based closely on the model of Christ and on Biblical imagery of destruction and revelation, he wrote: "You wake from dreams of doom and—for a moment—you know: beyond all the noise and the gestures, the only real thing, love's calm unwavering flame in the half-light of early dawn." And then, in a more specifically Biblical reference to John: "It *is* expedient for us, that one man should die for the people, and the whole nation perish not." And finally in his own poetry:

The gate opens: dazzled
I see the arena
Then I walk out naked
To meet my death . . .
I have watched the others:
Now I am the victim,
Strapped fast to the altar
For sacrifice.

Hammarskjold identified constantly with the survivor state, and his image of sacrifice had to do with stemming the forces of apocalyptic destruction which impressed themselves so strongly upon him. Unusual circumstances surrounding his death—his seeking and carrying out in a very personal way an extremely dangerous mission close to a combat area, and his leaving a completed manuscript of *Markings* on his table prior to his departure for Africa—have led some to look upon his death as a form of suicide. Whether or not this interpretation is justified, one must suspect that his imagery of martyrdom in some degree propelled him to his death, that in some measure he sought the death he found. I mention Hammarskjold not for the purpose of passing anything like final judgment on either his life or his death, but rather to suggest the precariousness and paradox of end-of-the-world imagery in our time.

The problem, then, is not only calling forth end-of-the-world imagery but in some degree mastering it, giving it a place in our aesthetic and moral imagination. It is not only futile to try, as so much of the world does, to dismiss images of Hiroshima and Auschwitz from human consciousness. To attempt to do so is to deprive us of our own history, of what we are. In blocking our imaginations we impair our capacity to create the new forms we so desperately require. We need Hiroshima and Auschwitz, as we need Vietnam and our everyday lives, in all of their horror, to deepen and free that imagination for the leaps it must make. In the words of Roethke: "In a dark time the eye begins to see." The vision of death gives life. The vision of total annihilation makes it possible to imagine living under and beyond that curse.

CHAPTER 6

Forms of Revitalization

In times of relative equilibrium, a society's symbols and institutions provide comforting guidelines for inner experience as well as external behavior. But in times of severe historical dislocation, these institutions and symbols—whether having to do with worship, work, learning, punishment, or pleasure— lose their power and psychological legitimacy. We still live in them, but they no longer live in us. Or rather we live a half-life with one another.

The quest for images and symbols in new combination, for what might be called communal resymbolization, is precarious and threatening—so much so that it can itself be falsely viewed as the cause for the cultural breakdown everyone senses.

Feelings of disintegration and loss permeate contemporary life. We have seen this in the literature of survival examined in Chapter 5 and earlier in our discussion of the confusion that exists in all the social sciences, and particularly in psychological and psychiatric paradigms. But the phenomenon of which I speak extends far beyond the state of the human sciences: it affects us all at every level of our individual and collective existence.

Consider, for instance, the widespread inclination to name

135

and interpret the contemporary man or woman not in terms of what he or she might actually be but rather in terms of what *has been*—that is, in terms of what we have survived. We speak of ourselves as postmodern, postindustrial, posthistoric, postidentity, posteconomic, postmaterialist, posttechnocratic, and so forth. There are pitfalls in this way of naming the present (or the future) after what no longer is (or will be), but the terms have an authentic source in the sense of survivorship, present or anticipated, that so pervades our deepest image of ourselves.

In other writings I have emphasized the importance of holocaust in our symbolic vocabulary—of the recent past (Nazi death camps, Hiroshima and Nagasaki, Vietnam), the present (beginnings of massive starvation in Africa and on the Indian subcontinent), and the future (imagery of ultimate destruction by nuclear weapons, environmental pollution, or other means). Now we see the imagery of holocaust coming together with the experience of postmodern cultural breakdown: our loss of faith not so much in this symbol or that but in the entire intricate web of images, rituals, institutions, and material objects that make up any culture. The urgency of contemporary innovation stems from this sense of survival and loss at the most profound experiential level. I keep thinking of a more or less rhetorical question put to me recently by a thoughtful student: "Are four thousand years of human experience merely adding up to the capacity to repair a deficiency in a spaceship several million light-years from home?"

I mentioned in Chapter 2 the emergence of a Protean psychological style of flux and flow of the self, or self-process—of what the young call "goin' through the changes" in an interminable series of experiments and explorations of varying depth, each of which may be readily abandoned in favor of still another psychological quest. The Protean style is that of a survivor of the kinds of technological and cultural holocausts, real and anticipated, that hover around us.

The Protean process is a product of a convergence of history and evolution. The two have always intertwined: Darwin's message was that man emerged from other species in a historical process, and there has been no lack of evolutionary interpretations of history. But we tend to view evolution as prehistorical, and history as postevolutionary. The separation has been based upon our assumption of time scales which differ radically in their impact upon the human being. During a historical unit of a decade or a century, the human race was rarely changed in a fundamental way; an evolutionary unit of a millennium or more was required for that to be accomplished. But our present revolutionary technology and unprecedented historical velocity cast doubt upon that distinction. We sense, uneasily, our capacity to eliminate the human race in evolution no less than in history. And, short of extinction, we are increasingly aware of technical capabilities in altering human form—whether genetically or through organ exchange or mind influence—as never before.

Like so many of our boundaries, that between history and evolution is obscured rather than eradicated. As history and evolution converge, innovators embrace our new access (made possible by technology) to all forms ever known to human culture. Poised at a confusing and liberating psychic brink, ready to plunge wildly ahead in an unknowable process devoid of clear destination, people suddenly discover, swirling about, the total array of images created over the full course of their historical and evolutionary past. These images become an elusive form of psychic nutriment, to be ingested, metabolized, excreted, and, above all, built upon and recombined in some kind of vital process.

Richard Sennett has observed that when a machine's parts wear down, the machine cannot operate. "But," Sennett continues, "the essence of human development is that *growth* occurs when old routines break down, when old parts are no longer enough for the needs of the organism. This same kind of change, in a larger sphere, creates the phenomenon of history in a culture."[1] Death and loss can occasion profound research, re-creation, and renewal. But, for such transformation to occur, the relationship of man to machine and of man to work must be altered in the direction of organic growth.

This is Lewis Mumford's principle of transition from mechanism to organism. But something more is involved as well: social arrangements that permit and encourage technology to become part of the larger principle of imaginative transcendence.

Re-creating the Modes of Symbolic Immortality

Everywhere, men and women band together to confront the pervasive sense of "living deadness" emanating from holocaust, undigested change, large technobureaucracy, and, above all, the image of the machine. They seek new forms of connection, movement, and integrity around which to build new communities for living and working. One way to probe some of the fundamental dimensions of this process of communal resymbolization is to view it within a framework of shifting modes of symbolic immortality. I believe that the significance of contemporary social experiments can best be grasped within this larger quest not just for change but for a change in enduring connectedness and commitment, in relationship to contemporary paths to immortality.

The biological-biosocial mode is at issue in the new kinds of families and familylike structures now taking shape. A wide variety of experimental communal arrangements press toward new forms of biosocial continuity—toward new "tribes," a new "people," or at least new forms of community. These groups (sometimes but not always called communes) concern themselves with root psychobiological matters— organic food, greater sexual freedom, collective child-rearing, and spontaneity of mental and physical expression.

Observe the altered definitions of manhood and woman-hood taking shape not only in such experimental enclaves but throughout much of society. Within a single generation we have seen the virtually exclusive American male idea of the tough (even brutal), tight-lipped, fists-ready, physically powerful, hard, antiartistic, no-nonsense, highly competitive sexual conqueror give way to the gentle, open, noncombative, physically unimpressive, soft, aesthetic-minded, indirect and associative, noncompetitive, sexually casual self-explorer— with a variety of types in between. Similarly, the feminine ideal of the soft, compliant, self-sacrificing, family-oriented helpmate has given way to that of the aggressive, physically and psychically strong, self-expanding, liberation-oriented feminist. Much of the original hippie and Women's Libera-tion movements can be understood as exploration in broad-ened definitions of sex roles, so that one can be soft and ten-tative while still manly, hard and assertive while still wom-anly. This kind of experiment on the part of any of these groups must inevitably include excesses and absurdities. But in reaching for both the center and the periphery of maleness and femaleness there is a groping toward fundamental altera-tion of the biosocial mode of immortality.

There is, in other words, a biological base to Protean ex-perimentation. And the theme of community—of quest for biosocial continuity—becomes fundamental to all contempo-rary transformation. The struggle for "community control" is often a struggle for community itself, an effort to combine autonomy (over the most fundamental aspects of life) with lasting human connection.

Protean efforts at transformation are very active in the theological—or, more accurately, religious or spiritual—mode. This is evident in experiments with both social-activist and experiential-meditative forms of Christianity and Judaism, as well as with Buddhist, Hindu, and other Eastern religions. One can also point to revived interest in various premodern religiouslike rituals and superstitions—Eastern and Western astrological charts, the Chinese *Book of Changes* (*I Ching*), and tarot cards and other forms of fortunetelling.

Most commentary emphasizes the antirational nature of this embrace of seemingly primitive spirituality. Irrationality can indeed be present, especially for those who develop a preoccupation with charts and cards or feelings and vibes that excludes ideas, growth, and change. More characteristic, I believe, are the people who make forays in and out of these varied spiritual alternatives, as experiments in both knowing and feeling, in which one absorbs a fragment here, an image there, and maintains a sense of flow that is more consistent (more "stable") than the involvement with any one of them.

John S. Dunne, the distinguished Catholic theologian, posits as the new religion of our time "a phenomenon we might call 'passing over.'" Dunne describes this process as "a going over to the standpoint of another culture, another way of life, another religion, . . . followed by an equal and opposite process we might call 'coming back,' coming back with new insight to one's own culture, one's own way of life, one's own religion."[2] The process, and the new religion itself, are epitomized not by Jesus or any other founder of a world religion but by Gandhi, who followed such a trajectory from Hinduism to Christianity (and to some extent to Islam) and then back to Hinduism.

But even Gandhi, in the very focus of his faith, has a certain nostalgic ring for us. Could it be that the holy man and woman of our time have only begun to invent themselves? Perhaps these new spiritual leaders will not merely "pass over" and "come back" in that relatively ordered sequence. It may be that they will do so in a sustained, repeated, perhaps even endless process, in which spiritual depth no longer depends upon exclusive doctrine of any kind and realization combines "the principle of permanence" with that of continuing open search.

There is a darker side, however, to that same process. Considerable anxiety can be generated by the very multiplicity of possibilities in "passing over" and in the Protean style in general. That anxiety around diffuseness can in turn contribute to the kind of quest for certainty we now see so widely expressed in fundamentalist religious sects and various totalistic spiritual movements. Whether such sects and movements take on the rhetoric of fundamentalist Protestantism or of assimilated Hinduism, their manipulations of guilt, confession, and individual existence itself within an ever-narrowing psychological environment can render them caricatures of "the principle of permanence" they so avidly seek.

Whatever forms prophets and practices may take, we can be certain that we will be witnessing great waves of religious feeling. For what we call religion directs itself, at least at its best, to precisely the kinds of altered relationships to death and the continuity of life that occur during any historical turning point. But contemporary priests must look carefully at the stirrings within their churches and temples (and the much stronger religious expressions outside them). This kind of renewed religious feeling presses not toward the stability of denominations and orders but toward their overthrow, not toward orderly worship within existing social arrangements but toward forms of worship—of celebration and immortalization—that subvert the numbing pseudo-ritual of "normal religion" in favor of newly immortalizing visions.

The third mode, that of symbolic immortality via man's works, has been a crucial area of social preoccupation. Involved here is the disorganized but powerful critique now under way of all major social institutions: those within which one learns, is governed, judged, or punished, and, above all, finds significance. In the fundamental questions raised about universities and schools, political and judicial arrangements, intellectual disciplines and professional practices, there is a common overriding theme: the quest for significant work experience, both in immediate involvement and in a sense of the work's contribution to the continuing human enterprise. What we call work is a uniquely important boundary between self-process and social vision. Perhaps for the first time in history very large numbers of men and women are beginning to demand harmony and meaning at that boundary; to demand a reasonable equation between work and "works."

This fundamental relationship between work and symbolic immortality is typified in the passions of the "work commune" movement—small communities that permit pooling of professional, political and psychobiological experiments. In these and such related groups as radical institutes and radical caucuses in all the professional disciplines, there is not only a powerful transformative element but a conservative one as well. There is a determination to confront and thereby preserve a particular social or intellectual tradition—rather than dismiss or ignore it—in a spirit critical both of the tradition itself and of its conventional applications.

This task of resymbolization, traditionally the mission of great innovators, has now become something close to a mass experience. Large numbers of people, in one way or another, move (in Daniel Berrigan's phrase) "toward the edge" of their profession or craft. They do so not necessarily because that was their original plan but because their immediate situation, which they can scarcely avoid confronting, evokes altered relationships and judgments. The ethical compromises and hypertrophied technical components of work and life, the nature of the society and culture in and for which one works—these raise inner questions about commitments to self and to vocation.

These questions and confrontations are part of a largely inchoate, yet profound, quest for newly immortalizing combinations of human influence. We may suspect that the structures and institutions that emerge will have to build into their own evolving tradition the expectation of the unexpected, the capacity to engender a stability in equilibrium with periodic transformation—which may, indeed, be the only form of true stability possible.

The natural mode of immortality has obvious relationship to ecological passions and to general fears about destruction of the environment, fears all too appropriate. But these passions and fears can connect with a more positive impulse toward nature, as exemplified by the rural commune (and simply rural-return) movement. Many have ridiculed this movement and have looked upon it as nothing more than a pathetic form of pastoral romanticism, a regression to a discredited myth that is particularly misdirected in our present urban-technological society. There is no doubt that many of these communal efforts *have* been romantically envisioned and poorly planned. Moreover, there is pathos and error in the claim occasionally made that they are *the* answer to our urban-technological dilemmas. But what is often missed in these exchanges is the psychological significance of reclaiming a relationship to nature as part of more general psychic renewal.

When young, and often not so young, Americans create a rural commune in New Mexico or New Hampshire, they approach nature with contemporary sensibilities. They seek to bring nature back into a meaningful cosmology, back into the human imagination. They embrace nature in an experiment with the self. The ramifications of that experiment may yet make their way into the most urban minds.

The final mode, that of experiential transcendence, differs from the others in being a psychic state *per se*. It includes various forms of ecstasy and rapture associated with the Dionysian principle of excess, and with the mystical sense of oneness with the universe Freud referred to as the "oceanic feeling." Mystics speak of a state of awareness in which, totally unencumbered by any particular idea or image, one is able to perceive the entirety of the larger universe and of one's own being within it.

This is the "high" one can get from drugs, or from various forms of intense encounter; the "trip"; the state of being "stoned." The terms are interesting. "High" implies elevation of psychic state in the direction of transcendence. "Trip" implies being in motion but something briefer and more temporary than, say, a "journey," and having the implicit suggestion of quick return. "Stoned" implies an absolute intensity (the smoothness, hardness, solidity, and finality of stone), in this case intensity of feeling, ecstasy—but also the numbness, insensitivity, or deadness of a stone (stone blind, stone deaf, stone dumb, stone cold, stone dead).

The duality in the term "stoned" may be appropriate. One undergoes a "small death" (of more or less ordinary feeling) in order to open oneself up to a "new life" (to feeling on a different plane of intensity), to a sense of transcendence. One becomes impervious to the prosaic idea of mortality and feels oneself so exquisitely attuned to, and indeed at times merged with, the universe as a whole that the issue of life versus death is no longer of consequence. Should the process fail, whether because of depending too much upon the technology of becoming "stoned" (the drugs themselves) or for other reasons, one is left in a state of perpetual numbing (stone dumb, stone cold, etc.).

In a wide variety of experiments—sexual, political, aesthetic—there is a powerful insistence upon making the quality of "awareness" or transcendence basic to the act. Indeed, there is a very real sense in which experiential transcendence is the key, the baseline, for the other four modes. That is, one requires some form of ecstasy and oneness—whether all-consuming or of a more gentle variety—in order to experience oneself as living on in one's children, works, spirituality, or relationship to nature. And that level of experience is also required for the inner psychological reordering necessary to individual transformation.

Transformation is achieved only by touching what I called in Chapter 3 the formative zone of the psyche. One might also speak of the mythic zone, as it is very close to what Mircea Eliade writes of as "the zone of the sacred, the zone of absolute reality." For the seeker, it is "the road to the self, the road to the 'center' of his being." The principle is one of psychic action, by which I mean the genuine inner contact leading to confrontation, reordering, and renewal. In describing ancient rituals surrounding the new year, one experiences (in Eliade's words) "the presence of the dead," the ceremonial depiction of "a 'death' and a 'resurrection,' a 'new birth,' a 'new man,'" and the overall principle that "life cannot be restored but only re-created."[3] This too is the principle of genuine Protean transformation.

But of course the difficulties in the path of psychological and social transformation are profound. For those moving into adulthood, the newness and instability of the contemporary situation are such that there can be few "formative fathers" and mothers available to emulate. Those who do exist are likely to be approached with a tenuous ambivalence or equally tenuous romanticism.

Apart from models or leaders, there are very few existing social institutions within which fundamental transformations can be explored or developed. The result is a form of floating confusion that is in turn related to profound difficulties in connecting innovation with a sense of actuality. The innovator is thus likely to fluctuate between extreme self-doubt and a seemingly opposite but psychologically related self-righteous moralism that claims dominion over truth.

Issues of betrayal and self-betrayal confront the innovator at every point. In the effort to change one "betrays" one's family and past; in the failure to take a particular leap or in the tendency to remain associated with existing society one "betrays" one's new associates in innovation. One experiences the guilt of social breakdown, the self-condemnation of the man without anything to be loyal to.

Most of all, the Protean experimenter must call forth dark areas of the psyche, demonic imagery of destruction and suffering as threatening to oneself as to society. These "death sources" both reflect the degree of personal dislocation and energize the renewal. While the more conventional person erects protective devices to avoid confronting individual and collective death imagery, the innovator moves toward this imagery, sensing like the artist that the new forms depend upon it. And today that confrontation must take place within the precarious diversity of the Protean pattern. No wonder young innovators ask the question, as one did of me, "In order to make revolution do you have to destroy yourself?"

To grasp some of the complex relationship between would-be innovators and their society, one must consider the theme of the "underground." One thinks of underground movements, especially in the political realm, as those relegated to a secret, invisible place by their very illegitimacy—by their unacceptability to those in control of society. For some groups such a definition undoubtedly still holds. But in broader present usage the theme of the underground may have greater importance as a psychic and social realm sought out by innovators in order to experiment with the work of transformation. Hence the word becomes almost interchangeable with "free" or "alternative"—and we have the underground church, the underground press, underground films, free or alternative schools, the free university, etc.

One should not be misled by the short life of most underground institutions or their confused and precarious relationship to and frequent absorption by the "overground" of proper society. We will continue to need underground themes in our society—imagery of a subterranean realm of both exquisite mysteries and terrible demons—a realm signifying the unconscious mind in Freud's sense and a land of death and continuous life in the paradigm I am suggesting. Our social critics often announce the death of the avant-garde, the counterculture, and the underground. But we can expect continuous psychic experimentation in that realm, with individuals and groups periodically emerging from it renewed by insight and vision with which to confront the formative zone of the larger society.

The ultimate task of transformation is the re-creation of the adult self. In significant degree, an adult is one who has ceased to play and begun to work. Of course adults play, too, but their play tends to be in the service of maintaining the social order as opposed to the spontaneous subversiveness of the play of children. Adult work is the work of culture; everyday tasks are conducted under the guiding principles of the culture's assumptions about transcendence and are subservient to the prevailing modes of immortality. Each steel girder installed, each mile driven in a taxi, each product-order typed and approved contributes to a culture's collective effort to cope with individual mortality through lasting enterprises, structures, and sequences.

Adult work is always tied in with a larger spiritual principle—whether that principle is the Protestant ethic, the deification of capital, or the revolutionary vision. Indeed, one way of defining adulthood is as a state of maximum absorption in everyday tasks subsumed to transcendent cultural principles, permitting minimal awareness of the threat of individual death. This is in contrast to both old age and youth. In old age one is impinged upon by the imminence of death and becomes preoccupied with immediate evidence of continuity and integrity, while in youth one requires more intense and direct modes of transcendence rather than the more indirect workaday kind.

When the young are accused of refusing to grow up and become adults there is a sense in which the accusation is true. Indeed, it must be true for innovators during any period of radical dislocation and change. What they reject is the existing version of adult existence. They sense that adulthood is a locked-in, desensitized state, one of unquestioned assumptions about work and productivity, family and other human relationships, and of fuzzy, nonviable, half-religious images about death, life, and "ultimate meaning."

Contemporary innovators seek a form of adulthood with more play in it. Play and playfulness are central not only to the kind of adulthood envisioned but to the process of change itself on the way to that state. (State and process, of course, merge.) Great innovators have always been able to play and, in many cases, have come to their innovations via elaborate and disciplined forms of play. While this play draws heavily upon childhood experience, it is nonetheless the play of adults, playfulness seasoned by form and accessible to insight. The innovator has always lived in exquisite equilibrium between a refusal to be an adult as ordinarily defined and a burdensome assumption of responsibility for a large segment of adult action and imagination. We sense now a demand that all, whatever their innovative talents, share in this playfulness and Proteanism until "adulthood" either disappears entirely or is renewed and transformed.

Ultimately, genuine transformation requires that we "experience" our annihilation in order to prevent it, that we confront and conceptualize both our immediate crises and our long-range possibilities for renewal. Joseph Campbell reminds us that "the idea of death and rebirth . . . is an extremely ancient one in the history of culture," frequently in the form of "a shock treatment for no longer wanted personality structure."[4] In our present Protean environment the principle still holds: *every significant step in human existence involves some inner sense of death.* As Francis Huxley puts the matter, "Where there is anxiety—as there is in every human culture—the imagination is called upon to destroy it by an act of reconstruction."[5] Destruction and reconstruction—death and rebirth in the quest for immortalizing connectedness—are at the center of man's creation of culture. From this process alone can the urgently needed transformation of our own culture ensue. Heinrich Böll tells us that "an artist always carries death with him like a good priest his breviary." The priest, the artist, the human being within us requires that we do no less.

CHAPTER 7

Advocacy: The Person in the Paradigm

In looking at the professions one does well to hold to the old religious distinction between the ministerial and the prophetic. One should not assume, as many do, a simple polarity in which the sciences are inherently radical or revolutionary and the healing professions intrinsically conservative. The professions must minister to people, take care of them, and that is a relatively conservative process. But there are prophets who emerge from the healing ministrations of the professions—Freud is a notable example—with radical critiques and revolutionary messages. Moreover, even "pure scientists" (in biology or physics, for example) spend most of their time ministering to the existing paradigm, doing what Thomas Kuhn calls "normal science," and strongly resist the breakthrough that is inevitably charted by the prophets among them. There are ministerial and prophetic elements in both the healing professions and the sciences.

But one must also distinguish between the professions, which have profound value in their capacity for continuity and renewal, and professionalism, the ideology of profes-

151

sional omniscience, which in our era inevitably leads to technicism and the model of the machine. The necessity for such a distinction becomes painfully clear if one looks at the situation that prevailed for psychiatrists in Vietnam. That situation can provide a starting point for a broader discussion of these dilemmas and their moral and conceptual ramifications in relation to the question of advocacy. In such extreme situations the professional may be no better able than his soldier patient to sort out the nuances of care and professional commitment on the one hand and moral (or immoral) action on the other.

I would suggest that those of us in the psychological professions have "survived" not only the collapse or threatened collapse of various theoretical paradigms. The Vietnam experience makes it clear that we have also "outlived" the period of ethical neutrality in the professions, the possibility of regarding our work and our place in society as being beyond moral scrutiny.[1] For us, as for others in similar situations, there are two general survivor alternatives: one can retreat from the issue raised by the death immersion and thereby remain bound to it in a condition of stasis and numbing; or one can confront the death immersion and derive insight and illumination from the overall survivor experience.[2] The latter response to some form of survival has probably been the source of most great religious and political movements, and of many breakthroughs in professional life as well.

Our own sense of survival, then, becomes inseparable from questions of advocacy (in both investigation and therapy) and of professional renewal. These and related ethical issues become especially prominent in relationship to an "extreme situation" such as the Vietnam War. But depth psychology has a tradition of great importance, much evident in Freud, of studying extremes in order to illuminate the more obscure features of the ordinary.

Freud's own advocacies have been summed up by Rieff in a single sentence: "For humanists in science, and for scientists of the human, Freud should be the model of a concern with the distinctly human that is truly scientific."[3] Within his ideal of the human-centered triumph of reason, Freud's "subversiveness" lay in his insistence upon radical truth (mostly about our sexual natures) and radical honesty in investigating and reporting that truth. His advocacy concerning sexuality itself was by no means that of simple license or even of "sexual revolution." Rather, his goal was the freeing of sexual feeling from the repressive mechanisms that, in his judgment, so impaired psychic and physical health. More broadly, the struggle was against the inordinate hypocrisies, sexual and otherwise, of his time and place.

Freud's scientific advocacy consisted of applying the Enlightenment quest for knowledge to the self—or, one might say, extending the Enlightenment into the self. Unfortunately but quite understandably (given the opposition Freud aroused and the precariousness of his undertaking), Freud came to equate these intellectual and moral advocacies with advocacy of the psychoanalytic *movement*. That is, his sense of immortality became bound up simultaneously with his fundamental ideas (especially as expressed in the sexual theory of neurosis and in his book *The Interpretation of Dreams*) and with the institution he spawned. He came to stress the consolidation of both theoretical and institutional structure. It would have been indeed difficult for him to have stressed instead "permanent revolution"—but had he been able to do that, with psychoanalysis as idea and institution, subsequent psychological work and thought would have been much better served.[4]

Politically and socially, Freud's advocacy was somewhere in the libertarian tradition of John Stuart Mill, whom he admired as "perhaps the man of the century who best managed

to free himself from the domination of customary prejudices."
As a young man, Freud had translated Mill, though he was
critical of Mill's "lifeless style" and "prudish . . . ethereal"
tone. He especially faulted Mill on "the woman's question,"
about which Freud himself took a conventional, chivalric-
patriarchal view. Freud thought Mill unrealistic in under-
estimating the extent to which (in Freud's view) managing a
home and bringing up children demand "the whole of a human being."⁵ His conservative cast was associated with his
view of human nature as virtually unchanging and of history
as essentially cyclic. He was thus deeply skeptical not only
of utopian political projects but of moral progress in general.
One must therefore say that the present situation of psychoanalysis in being so frequently associated with defense of the
status quo has at least a beginning in Freud, but so does its
more radical potential for allying itself with all varieties of
human liberation.

Erik Erikson's central advocacy can be described as the
realization of the life cycle in the achievement of individual
and collective modes of harmony. To this end he favors and
projects ever more inclusive forms of identity. He sees his
work (rightly, I believe) as addressing some of the fundamental threats to human survival we now experience. This is
directly evident in his study of Gandhi and nonviolence, and
more indirectly in his concern with optimal psychological
conditions for human development. In association with the
stages of the life cycle, Erikson presents what he calls the
"basic virtues": hope, will, purpose, and competence during
childhood; fidelity during adolescence; and love, care, and
wisdom during adulthood.⁶ Erikson is, like Freud, libertarian
in spirit, but perhaps more sympathetic than Freud to modes
of unconventionality generally associated with the "artistic

temperament" (his own and others). It is nonetheless significant that Erikson, during a period of great upheaval in the
United States, has generally avoided direct political and social commitments. He did take an important stand during
the McCarthyite period of the mid-1950s in refusing to sign a
loyalty oath (thereby having to leave the University of California). Like the great majority of intellectuals in America,
he opposed the Vietnam War. But his strongest public stand
during the last two decades or so has been one of reconcilia-
tion: the endorsement, together with a group of other prominent Americans, of amnesty for war resisters.

In a manner quite different from Erikson and Freud, I
have been actively involved in oppositional political struggles,
especially the anti–Vietnam War and anti–nuclear-weapons
movements. These involvements have closely paralleled my
investigative preoccupations with what I take to be the special historical features of our era—its possibilities for near-
total self-annihilation as well as its impulses toward fundamental kinds of transformation. Beginning with my work in
Hiroshima, I have come to see advocacy itself as having a
necessary ethical and conceptual place in the healing professions. In my more recent study of antiwar Vietnam veterans I joined their crusade against the war as a way of continuing my own protest. But I also endeavored to stand back
from it and them sufficiently to interpret their psychological
experiences. I sought to combine detachment sufficient to enable me to make psychological evaluations (which I had to
do at every step) with involvement that expressed my own
commitments and moral passions. We in the psychological
professions always function within this dialectic between
ethical involvement and intellectual rigor, and I believe that
bringing our advocacy "out front" and articulating it makes

us more, rather than less, scientific. Indeed, our scientific accuracy is likely to suffer when we hide our ethical beliefs behind the claim of neutrality. I view this dialectic of advocacy and detachment (again, Buber's distance and relation) to have great importance, even in the most "clinical" of situations.*[7]

The work with Vietnam veterans grew out of prior antiwar advocacy and professional concern with holocaust deriving from my research in Hiroshima. I participated, along with other psychological professionals, in a program of "rap groups" with antiwar veterans between 1971 and 1974. I want to describe some of the features of those groups and conclude with more general observations in relation to the problem of advocacy in psychological and psychiatric work.

The veterans' rap groups came into being because the veterans sensed that they had more psychological work to do in connection with the war.[8] It is important to emphasize that the veterans themselves initiated the groups. The men knew that they were "hurting," but did not want to seek help from the Veterans Administration, which they associated with the military, the target of much of their rage. But though they knew they were in psychological pain, they did not consider themselves patients. They wanted to understand what they had been through, begin to heal themselves, and at the same time make known to the American public the human costs of the war. These two aspects of the veterans' aspirations in forming the groups—healing themselves while finding a mode of political expression—paralleled the professional dialectic of rigor and advocacy mentioned earlier. Without using those words, the veterans had that combination very much in mind when they asked me to work with them.

* Ronald Laing, for instance, has been both advocate and interpreter of the person we call schizophrenic, no less than I of antiwar veterans, though obviously in different and less overtly "political" ways.

From the beginning we avoided a medical model: we called ourselves "professionals" rather than "therapists" (the veterans often referred to us simply as "shrinks"), and we spoke of rap groups rather than group therapy. We were all on a first-name basis, and there was a fluidity in the boundaries between professionals and veterans. But the boundaries remained important nonetheless. Distinctions remained important to both groups, and in the end the healing role of professionals was enhanced by the extent to which veterans could become healers in relationship to one another and, in some degree, to professionals also. Equally important, there was an assumption, at first unspoken and later articulated, that everybody's life was at issue. Professionals in the group had no special podium from which to avoid self-examination. We too could be challenged, questioned about anything. All of this seemed natural enough to the veterans, but it was a bit more problematic for the professionals. As people used to interpreting others' motivations, it was at first a bit jarring for us to be confronted with hard questions about our own, and with challenges about the way we lived. Our willingness to share this kind of involvement was crucial to the progress of the group, and in the end many of us among the professionals came to value and enjoy it.

As in certain parallel experiments taking place not only in psychological work but throughout American culture, we had a clearer idea of what we opposed (hierarchical distancing, medical mystification, psychological reductionism that undermines political and ethical ideas) than of what we favored as specific guidelines. But before long I came to recognize three principles that seemed important. The first is *affinity*, the coming together of people who share a particular (in this case overwhelming) historical or personal experience. The members of the group share some fundamental perspective, and come together to make sense of their experience. The second principle is *presence,* a kind of being-there or full engagement and openness to mutual impact. No one in such a group is simply a neutral therapist against whom ideas and emotions merely rebound. The third principle is *self-generation,* the need on the part of those seeking help, change, or insight of any kind to initiate their own process and conduct it largely on their own terms. Even when calling in others with expert knowledge, they retain major responsibility for the shape and direction of the enterprise. Affinity, presence, and self-generation seem to be necessary ingredients for making a transition between old and new images and values. These are particularly significant when the issues at stake relate to ultimate concerns, to shifting modes of historical continuity and symbolic immortality.

I do not want to give the impression that everything went smoothly. There were a number of tensions in the group, one of them having to do with its degree of openness and fluidity. Openness was an organizing principle: in the fashion of "street-corner psychiatry," any Vietnam veteran was welcome to join a group at any time. Fluidity was dictated by the life styles of many of the veterans, who traveled extensively around the country and did not hold regular jobs. Professionals too were unable to attend every session. We established a policy of assigning three professionals to a group, with arrangements that at least one come to each meeting— but professionals became so involved in the process that there were usually two or all three present.

There was a tension among the professionals between two views of what we were doing. In the beginning a majority of the professionals felt that the essential model for our group sessions was that of group therapy. These professionals argued that the men were suffering and needed help and that if we as therapists offered anything less than group therapy we were denying them what they most needed. I held to a second model which was at first a minority view. This position acknowledged the important therapeutic element of what we were doing, but emphasized the experimental nature of our work in creating a new institution and even a new community, however limited and temporary. From this perspective the groups furthered a sustained dialogue between professionals and veterans based on a common stance of opposition to the war in which both groups drew upon their own special knowledge, experience and needs. This model did not abolish role definitions: veterans were essentially there to be helped and professionals to help; but it placed more stress on mutuality and shared commitment.

We never totally resolved the tension between these two models in the sense of coming to share a single position. The veterans tended to favor the second model, but did not want to be short-changed in terms of help they wanted and needed. For both veterans and professionals there was a continuing dialectic between these two ways of seeing what we were doing. But those professionals who held to the second model—which related to other experiments taking place in American society with which the veterans identified—tended to stay longer with the project. Those professionals who conceived the effort in a more narrowly defined therapeutic way, and who, I suspect, were less politically and ethically committed to an antiwar position, tended to leave.

Of course, there were differences in professional style even within these two models. Some professionals were particularly skilled at uncovering the childhood origins of conflicts. I was seen as an authority on issues of death and life continuity and on social-historical dimensions around death and survival. In personal style, my impulse was to be something of a mediator, and the group soon came to see me in that way.

The group recognized and accepted these differing personal styles, and it was interesting to us as professionals to observe reflections of ourselves in the responses to us not only of veterans but of other professionals sharing the experience of a particular group.

The veterans began with almost no knowledge of group process, but they learned quickly. From the beginning the focus in the groups was on the overwhelming experience of the war and on residual guilt and rage. In the process of examining these issues the men looked increasingly at their ongoing life struggles, especially their relationships with women, feelings about masculinity, and conflicts around work. There was a back-and-forth rhythm in the group between immediate life situations and war-related issues. These gradually blended in the deepening self-examination that was generally associated in turn with social and political forces in the society.

For all of us in the group there was a sense that the combination of ultimate questions (around death and survival) and experimental arrangements required that we call upon new aspects of ourselves and become something more than we had been before. Central to this process was the changing relationship between veterans and professionals. At moments the veterans could become critical of the way professionals were functioning. There was one bitter expression of resentment by a veteran who felt that the interpretations made by a professional were too conventional and tended to ignore or undercut issues very important to him. The group discussed the matter at great length. I agreed in part with the veteran, but also tried to point out that the interpretation was made in good faith.

At another point, one of the veterans spoke very angrily to me because I was occupied with my note-taking. I was trying to record the words of the veterans precisely because, as we had discussed earlier, I was in the group not only as a healer but also as an investigator who would write about the experience. When we discussed the matter it became clear that the veterans had no difficulty accepting that dual role. What they objected to was my not being fully "present" in focusing on taking notes. After a bit of thought I decided they were right. I ceased my note-taking and from that point on made notes only at the end of each session, a well-established pattern in the practice of psychotherapy that I had to relearn. There were, of course, many other conflicts as well, but there was also an essential feeling of moving toward authentic insight. By taking seriously such issues as they were raised, we maintained a double level of individual-psychological interpretation and shared actuality that contributed to the sense of everyone's "presence."

The rap groups represented a struggle on the part of both veterans and psychological professionals to give form to what was in many ways a common survival, a survival for the veterans of a terrible death immersion and for the professionals of their own dislocations in relationship to the war and society. During our most honest moments we professionals have admitted that the experience has been as important for our souls as for theirs.

The rap groups have been one small expression (throughout the country they and related programs have probably involved, at most, a few thousand people) of a much larger cultural struggle I described in Chapter 6, toward creating animating institutions.[9] Whether these emerge from existing institutions significantly modified or as "alternative institutions," they can serve the important function of providing new ways of being a professional and of working with professionals. While such institutions clearly have radical possibilities, they can also serve a genuinely conservative function, as I suggested in regard to other work in the previous chapter. Such institutions enable those involved to find a means of continuing to relate, however critically, to existing social institutions, as opposed to retreating in embittered alienation, destructiveness, or self-destructiveness. In this and other ways, the rap-group experience seemed to me a mirror on psychohistorical struggles of considerable importance throughout the society.

Guilt and rage were fundamental emotions that we explored constantly in the groups.[10] The men had a special kind of anger best described as ironic rage toward two types of professionals with whom they came into contact in Vietnam: chaplains and "shrinks." They talked about chaplains with great anger and resentment as having blessed the troops, their mission, their guns, and their killing: "Whatever we were doing—murder, atrocities—God was always on our side." Catholic veterans spoke of having confessed to meaningless transgressions ("Sure, I'm smoking dope again, I guess I blew my state of grace again") while never being held accountable for the ultimate one ("But I didn't say anything about killing"). It was as if the chaplains were saying to them, "Stay within our moral clichés as a way of draining off excess guilt, and then feel free to plunge into the business at hand."

The men also pointed to the chaplains' even more direct role of promoting false witness. One man spoke especially bitterly of "chaplains' bullshit." He illustrated what he meant by recalling the death of a close buddy—probably the most overwhelming experience one can have in combat—followed by a combined funeral ceremony and pep talk at which the chaplain urged the men to "kill more of them." Another, who had carried the corpse of his closest buddy on his back after his company had been annihilated, described a similar ceremony at which the chaplain spoke of "the noble sacrifice for the sake of their country" made by the dead. It is not generally recognized that the My Lai massacre occurred immediately after the grotesque death from an exploding booby trap of a fatherly, much revered noncommissioned officer, which had been witnessed by many of the men. The funeral ceremony for the dead officer was conducted jointly by a chaplain and the commanding officer, the former lending spiritual legitimacy to the latter's mixture of eulogy and exhortation to "kill everything in the village." A eulogy in any funeral service asks those in attendance to carry forward the work of the person who died. In war that "work" characteristically consists of getting back at the enemy. A war funeral can thus provide men with a means of resolving survivor guilt by means of a "survivor mission" that involves a sense not only of revenge but of carrying forth the task the fallen comrade could not see to completion. In Vietnam, the combination of a hostile environment and the absence of an identifiable "enemy" led to the frequent manipulation of grief to generate a form of "false witness," a survivor mission of atrocity.[11]

The men spoke with the same bitterness about "shrinks" they had encountered in Vietnam. They described situations in which they or others experienced an overwhelming combination of psychological conflict and moral revulsion, difficult to distinguish in Vietnam. Whether one then got to see a chaplain, a psychiatrist, or an enlisted-man medic had to do with where one was at the time, who was available, and the attitudes of the soldier and the authorities in one's unit toward religion and psychiatry. But should a soldier succeed in seeing a psychiatrist, he was likely to be "helped" to remain on duty, to carry on with the daily commission of war crimes. For many ordinary GI's, psychiatry served to erode whatever capacity they retained for moral revulsion and animating guilt. In the rap groups the men talked about ways in which psychiatry became inseparable from military authority.

But in their resentment of chaplains and psychiatrists the men were saying something more. It was one thing to be ordered by command into a situation that one had come to perceive as both absurd and evil, but it was quite another to have that process rationalized and justified by ultimate authorities of the spirit and mind—that is, by chaplains and psychiatrists. One could even say that spiritual and psychological authority was employed to seal off in the men some inner alternative to the irreconcilable evil they were asked to embrace. In that sense the chaplains and psychiatrists formed an unholy alliance not only with the military command but also with the more corruptible elements in the soldier's psyche, corruptible elements available to all of us.

We can then speak of the existence of a "counterfeit universe" in which pervasive, spiritually reinforced inner corruption became the price of survival. In this sense, the chaplains and psychiatrists were just as entrapped as the GI's. For we may assume that most of them were reasonably conscientious and decent professionals caught up in an institutional commitment in this particular war.

When the men spoke harshly in our group about military psychiatrists we professionals of course asked ourselves whether they were talking about us. In some degree they undoubtedly were. They were raising the question whether *any* encounter with a psychiatrist, even in a context which they themselves created, and into which we were called, could be more authentic than the counterfeit moral universe that psychiatrists had lent themselves to in Vietnam.

In the rap-group experience I found the issue of investigative advocacy more pressing and powerful than in other research I have done. This was partly because veterans and professionals alike were more or less in the middle of the problem: the war continued, and we all had painful emotions about what it was doing, and what we were doing or not doing to combat it.* But I came to realize that, apart from the war, the work had important bearing upon a sense of long-standing crisis affecting all of us in the psychological professions and the professions in general—a crisis that the war in Vietnam both accentuated and illuminated but by no means created. We professionals came to the rap groups with our own need for transformations in ways parallel to, if more muted than, those which we sought to enhance in veterans. We too, sometimes with less awareness than they, were in the midst of struggles around living and working that had to do with intactness, wholeness, and integrity.

One source of perspective on that struggle was a return to the root ideas of profession, the idea of what it means to profess. Indeed, an examination of the evolution of these two words could provide something close to cultural history of the West. The prefix "pro" means forward, toward the front, forth, out, or into a public position. "Fess" derives from the Latin *fateri* or *fass*, meaning to confess, own, acknowledge. To profess (or be professed), then, originally meant a personal form of out-front public acknowledgment. And that which was acknowledged or "confessed" always (until the sixteenth century) had to do with religion: with taking the vows of a religious order or declaring one's religious faith. But as society became secularized, the word came to mean

---

* In contrast, my Hiroshima work, in which I also experienced strong ethical involvement, was retrospective and in a sense prospective (there were immediate nuclear problems, of course, but we were not in the midst of a nuclear holocaust); my study of Chinese thought reform dealt with matters of immediate importance but going on (in a cultural sense) far away; and my work with Japanese youth had much less to do with overwhelming threat and ethical crisis.[12]

"to make claim to have knowledge of an art or science" or "to declare oneself expert or proficient in" an enterprise of any kind. The noun form, "profession," came to suggest not only the act of professing but also the ordering, collectivization, and transmission of the whole process. The sequence was from "profession" or religious conviction (in the twelfth century) to a particular order of "professed persons," such as monks or nuns (fourteenth century), to "the occupation which one professes to be skilled in and follow," especially "the three learned professions of divinity, law, and medicine" along with the "military profession." So quickly did the connotations of specialization and application take hold that as early as 1605 Francis Bacon could complain: "Amongst so many great foundations of colleges in Europe, I find strange that they are all dedicated to professions, and none left free to Art and Sciences at large."[13]

Thus the poles of meaning around the image of profession shifted from the proclamation of personal dedication to transcendent principles to membership in and mastery of a specialized form of socially applicable knowledge and skill. In either case, the profession is immortalizing—the one through the religious mode, the other through works and social-intellectual tradition. And the principles of public proclamation and personal discipline carry over from the one meaning to the other—the former taking the shape of examination and licensing, the latter of study, training, and dedication. Overall, the change was from advocacy based on faith to technique devoid of advocacy.*

---

* One can observe this process in the modern separation of "profession" from "vocation." "Vocation" also has a religious origin in the sense of being "called by God" to a "particular function or station." The secular equivalent became the idea of a personal "calling" in the sense of overwhelming inclination, commitment, and even destiny. But the Latin root of "vocation," *vocare*, to call, includes among its meanings and derivatives: vocable, voca-

To be sure, contemporary professions do contain general forms of advocacy: in law, of a body of suprapersonal rules applicable to everyone; in medicine, of healing; and in psychiatry, of humane principles of psychological well-being and growth. But immediate issues of value-centered advocacy and choice (involving groups and causes served and consequences thereof) are mostly ignored. In breaking out of the premodern trap of immortalization by personal surrender to faith, the "professional" has fallen into the modern trap of pseudo-neutrality and covert immortalization of technique. As a result, our professions are all to ready to offer their techniques to anyone and anything. I am in no way suggesting a return to pure faith as a replacement for contemporary distortions around the idea of the professions. But I am convinced that we require a model of the "ethical professional" that includes issues of advocacy and commitment.

The psychiatrist in Vietnam, whatever his intentions, found himself in collusion with the military in conveying to individual GI's an overall organizational message: "Do your indiscriminate killing with confidence that you will receive expert medical-psychological help if needed." Keeping in mind Camus' warning that men should become neither victims nor executioners, this can be called—at least in Vietnam—the psychiatry of the executioner.[14] I do not exempt myself from this critique. I served as a military psychiatrist in the Korean War under conditions that had at least some parallels to those in

---

tion, vouch; advocate, advocation, convoke, evoke, invoke, provoke, and revoke. Advocacy is thus built into the original root and continuing feel of the word "vocation"; and "vocation," in turn, is increasingly less employed in connection with the work a man or woman does. If we do not say "profession," we say "occupation," which implies seizing, holding, or simply filling in space in an area of time; or else "job," a word of unclear origin that implies task, activity, or assignment that is, by implication, self-limited or possibly part of a larger structure, including many related jobs, but not, in essence, related to an immortalizing tradition or principle.

Vietnam. And although I had very little to do with men in combat, it is quite possible that my work since has been affected by that personal "survival."

The military's approach to psychiatry emphasizes "the therapeutic endeavor . . . to facilitate the men's integration into their own groups (units) through integration into the group of ward patients."[15] The approach seems convincing until one evaluates some of the conditions under which atrocities occurred or were avoided. I spent ten hours interviewing a man who had been at My Lai and had not fired or even pretended he was firing. (Among the handful who did not fire, most held their guns in position as if firing in order to avoid the resentment of the majority actively participating in the atrocity.) Part of what sustained this man and gave him the strength to risk ostracism was his very distance from the group. Always a "loner," he had, as a child raised beside the ocean, engaged mainly in such solitary activities as boating and fishing. Hence, though an excellent soldier, he was less susceptible than others to group influence, and in fact remained sufficiently apart from other men in his company to be considered "maladapted" to that immediate group situation.[16]

One must distinguish between group integration and integrity—the latter including moral and psychological elements that connect one to social and historical contexts beyond the immediate. Group integration can readily undermine integrity—in Vietnam for both soldiers and psychiatrists who had to grapple with their own struggles to adapt to a military institution with its goals of maximum combat strength, and to a combat situation of absurdity and evil. The psychiatrist, no less than the combat soldier, is confronted with important questions about the group he is to serve and, above all, the nature and consequences of its immediate and long-range mission. To deal with that question he must overcome the technicist assumption one falls into all too easily: "Because I am a healer, anything I do, anywhere, is good."

A formative perspective, a focus on images and forms and on their continuous development and re-creation, gives the psychiatrist a way of addressing historical forces without neglecting intrapsychic concerns. The antiwar passions of a particular Vietnam veteran, for instance, had to be understood as a combined expression of many different psychic images and forms: the Vietnam environment and the forces shaping it; past individual history; the post-Vietnam American experience, including Vietnam Veterans Against the War and the rap groups and the historical forces shaping these; and the various emanations of guilt, rage, and altered self-process that could and did take shape. Moreover, professionals like myself, who entered into the lives of these veterans, with our own personal and professional histories and personal struggles involving the war, became a part of the overall image-form constellation.

Psychiatrists have a great temptation to swim with an American tide that grants them considerable professional status but resists, at times quite fiercely, serious attempts to alter existing social and institutional arrangements. As depth psychologists and psychoanalysts, we make a kind of devil's bargain that we can plunge as deeply as we like into intrapsychic conflicts while not touching too critically upon historical dimensions that question those institutional arrangements. We often accept this dichotomy quite readily with the rationale that we are not, after all, historians or sociologists. But the veterans' experience shows that one needs extrospection as well as introspection to deal with psychological conflicts, particularly at a time of rapid social change. I believe that a general psychological paradigm of "death and the continuity of life" helps one to attain this dual perspective, and to recognize the interplay of psychological and moral elements in relationship to ultimate commitments.

All this points toward the need for a transformation of the healing professions themselves. At the end of Chapter 4 I mentioned a model of change, based on a sequence of confrontation, reordering, and renewal, which was important in my work with veterans. I think this model can be helpful to us in the healing professions to begin to examine ourselves.

For the veterans, confrontation meant confronting the idea of dying in Vietnam, often through the death of a buddy. For psychiatrists it would mean confronting our own concerns about death, mortality and immortality, and our personal and professional struggles with them. Reordering for the veterans meant the working through of difficult emotions around guilt and rage; for psychiatry this would mean seeking animating relationships to the same emotions in ourselves and recognizing and making use of our experience of despair.[17] Renewal for veterans meant a new sense of self and world, including an enhanced playfulness. The professional parallels are there as well, and much can be said for the evolution of more playful modes of investigation and therapy.

The urgency of our situation in the professions is suggested by the experiments which Stanley Milgram has conducted on the whole issue of obedience to authority.[18] The experiments focused specifically on the willingness of people to cause pain and even to endanger the lives of others, when authoritatively requested to do so. Whatever one's view of the scientific and moral aspects of these "Eichmann experiments," one of Milgram's own conclusions is worth thinking about: "Men are doomed if they act only within the alternatives handed down to them."

But if there is a compelling moral urgency that must be

confronted, there is also a pervasive confusion that is no less difficult to resolve. That is why I believe we must call forth the ethos of the survivor as we sense the "passing" of a psychological "way of life." For that is exactly what a change in paradigm means. There will be those who see no "momentous shift" or no shift at all. And there will be others who will find little of value in any of the three paradigms I have described. My work has taught me that in every form of survivor experience there is considerable possibility for avoidance, numbing, and stasis. But there is also possibility for confrontation, enhanced sensitivity, and renewal. Only the latter course does honor to our mentors and to ourselves. For: "A god outgrown becomes immediately a life-destroying demon. The form has to be broken and the energies released."[19]

Notes

Chapter 1 (pages 21–28)

1. Thomas S. Kuhn, *The Structure of Scientific Revolutions* (Chicago: Univ. of Chicago Press, 1962, 1970 [2nd edition]), postscript, p. 175. The remaining quotations in this and the next two paragraphs are from the same Kuhn volume.
2. Harry Guntrip, "Science, Psychodynamic Reality and Autistic Thinking," *Journal of the American Academy of Psychoanalysis*, Vol. I, No. 1, pp. 3-22, 7.
3. Gerald Holton, *Thematic Origins of Scientific Thought: Kepler to Einstein* (Cambridge, Mass.: Harvard Univ. Press, 1973).
4. Robert Jay Lifton, *Death in Life* (New York: Random House, 1968; Touchstone paperback, 1976), pp. 540-41.
5. See Ernst Cassirer, *An Essay on Man* (Doubleday Anchor, 1944), *The Myth of the State* (Doubleday Anchor, 1946), and *The Philosophy of Symbolic Forms*, 3v. (New Haven: Yale Univ. Press, 1953–57); and Susanne K. Langer, *Philosophy in a New Key* (Cambridge, Mass.: Harvard Univ. Press, 1942), *Feeling and Form* (New York: Scribner's, 1953), *Philosophical Sketches* (Baltimore: Johns Hopkins Press, 1962), and *Mind: An Essay on Human Feeling*, 2v. (Baltimore: Johns Hopkins Press, 1967–72; Vol. III in preparation).

Chapter 2 (pages 29–47)

1. Sigmund Freud, "Thoughts for the Times on War and Death," *Standard Edition of the Complete Psychological Works of Sigmund Freud*, ed. James Strachey (London: Hogarth Press, 1953–66), Vol. XIV, p. 289.
2. Carl Jung, *Modern Man in Search of a Soul* (New York: Harcourt Brace, 1936), p. 129.
3. Avery Weisman and Thomas Hackett, "Predilection to Death: Death and Dying as a Psychiatric Problem," *Psychosomatic Medicine*, Vol. XXXIII, No. 3 (May–June 1961).

4. Otto Rank, *Beyond Psychology* (New York: Dover reprint, 1958), p. 64.
5. Leslie Farber, "The Therapeutic Despair," *The Ways of the Will* (New York/London: Basic Books, 2nd printing, 1966).
6. Marghanita Laski, *Ecstasy: A Study of Some Secular and Religious Experiences* (Bloomington: Indiana Univ. Press, 1961).
7. Mircea Eliade, *Cosmos and History: The Myth of the Eternal Return* (New York: Torchbooks, 1959).
8. Lifton, *Revolutionary Immortality: Mao Tse-tung and the Chinese Cultural Revolution* (New York: Random House, 1968; Norton Library paperback, 1976), p. 10.
9. Kenneth Boulding, *The Image* (Ann Arbor: Univ. of Michigan Press, 1956).
10. John Bowlby, *Attachment and Loss*, Vol. I: *Attachment* (New York: Basic Books, 1969).
11. Melanie Klein *et al.*, *Developments in Psychoanalysis* (London: Hogarth Press, 1952).
12. Kenneth Keniston, *Young Radicals* (New York: Harcourt Brace Jovanovich, 1968).
13. Robert Jay Lifton, "Protean Man," *Partisan Review*, Vol. XXXV, No. 1 (Winter 1968), pp. 13-27; *Boundaries: Psychological Man in Revolution* (New York: Random House, 1970; Touchstone paperback, 1976), pp. 37-63; and *Archives of General Psychiatry*, Vol. XXIV, April 1971, pp. 298-304.
14. Erik H. Erikson, *Childhood and Society* (New York: Norton, 1950).
15. See also Lifton, *Home from the War: Vietnam Veterans, Neither Victims nor Executioners* (New York: Simon and Schuster, 1973).
16. Joseph D. Teicher, " 'Combat Fatigue' or 'Death Anxiety Neurosis,' " *Journal of Nervous and Mental Disease*, Vol. 117 (1953), pp. 232-42.
17. Abram Kardiner, "Traumatic Neuroses of War," *American Handbook of Psychiatry*, Vol. I (1959), pp. 246-57.
18. Wilhelm Stekel, *Nervous Anxiety States and Their Treatment*, transl. Rosalie Gabler (New York: Dodd, Mead and Co., 1923), as cited in Jacques Choron, *Modern Man and Mortality* (New York: Macmillan, 1964), p. 131.
19. Rank, *Will Therapy* (New York: Knopf, 1950).
20. Freud, *Civilization and Its Discontents*, in *Standard Edition*, Vol. XXI, p. 89.
21. Lifton, *The Broken Connection*, ms., chapter on "Death and Psychiatry."

22. Colin Murray Parkes, *Bereavement: Studies of Grief in Adult Life* (New York: International Universities Press, 1972).
23. George R. Crupp and Bernard Kligfeld, "The Bereavement Reaction: A Cross Cultural Evaluation," *Journal of Religion and Health*, Vol. I (1962), pp. 222-46.
24. Freud, "Analysis of a Phobia in a Five-Year-Old Boy," *Standard Edition*, Vol. X, pp. 5-149.
25. Harold Searles, "Schizophrenia and the Inevitability of Death," *Psychiatric Quarterly*, Vol. XXXV (1961), pp. 631-35.
26. R. D. Laing, *The Divided Self* (Baltimore: Penguin [Pelican], 1965), p. 176.
27. Primo Levi, *Survival in Auschwitz* (New York: Collier, 1961), p. 82.
28. See, for instance, various papers in Don B. Jackson, ed., *The Etiology of Schizophrenia* (New York: Basic Books, 1960).
29. *Ibid.*

Chapter 3 (pages 49–81)

1. Ernest Jones, *The Life and Work of Sigmund Freud* (New York: Basic Books, 1953), Vol. I, p. 348.
2. Josef Breuer and Sigmund Freud, "Studies in Hysteria," in Sigmund Freud, *Standard Edition of the Complete Psychological Works*, Vol. II (London: Hogarth Press, 1955), pp. 21-47.
3. Jones, Vol. I, pp. 319-24; and Max Schur, *Freud: Living and Dying* (New York: International Universities Press, 1972), pp. 93-152.
4. Freud, "New Introductory Lectures on Psycho-Analysis," in Hinsie and Campbell, *Psychiatric Dictionary*, 3rd edition (New York: Oxford Univ. Press, 1960), p. 422.
5. Erik H. Erikson, "Autobiographic Notes on the Identity Crisis," *Daedalus*, Fall 1970, pp. 730-59. Most biographical details mentioned below are from this essay.
6. Erik H. Erikson, *Young Man Luther* (New York: Norton, 1958) and *Gandhi's Truth* (New York: Norton, 1969).
7. See especially *Gandhi's Truth*, "Prologue: Echoes of an Event," pp. 19-52; and "On the Nature of Psycho-Historical Evidence: In Search of Gandhi," *Daedalus*, Summer 1968, pp. 695-730.
8. Erikson, "Autobiographic Notes," *loc. cit.*
9. Erikson, *Childhood and Society* (New York: Norton, 1950), *Identity and the Life Cycle* (New York: International Universities Press, Psychological Issues, Vol. I, No. 1, 1959), and *Identity: Youth and Crisis* (New York: Norton, 1968).

10. Erikson, *Gandhi's Truth*, p. 417. Subsequent quotations are from pp. 423-36.
11. Lifton, *Revolutionary Immortality*.
12. Lifton, *Death in Life*, "Introduction: Research and Researcher," p. 10.
13. Lifton, *History and Human Survival: Essays on the Young and the Old, Survivors and the Dead, Peace and War, and on Contemporary Psychohistory* (New York: Random House, 1970). See especially pp. 4-5 of "Introduction: On Becoming a Psychohistorian," pp. 3-21.
14. See also Lifton, *Death in Life;* and *Home from the War* (New York: Simon and Schuster, 1973).
15. Harry Guntrip, "Science, Psychodynamic Reality and Autistic Thinking," p. 20.
16. In letter to Frederik van Eeden, Dec. 28, 1914, in Schur, *op. cit.,* p. 293.
17. *The Future of an Illusion,* in *Standard Edition,* Vol. XXI, p. 53.
18. "New Introductory Lectures on Psycho-Analysis," *Standard Edition,* Vol. XXII, p. 80.
19. Ernest Jones, *Papers on Psycho-Analysis* (Baltimore: Wood, 1938), in Hinsie and Campbell, *Psychiatric Dictionary*, 3rd edition (New York: Oxford Univ. Press, 1960), p. 645.
20. Erikson, *Childhood and Society*, p. 207.
21. Lancelot Law Whyte, *The Next Development in Man* (New York: Mentor Books, 1949), *Accent on Form* (New York: Harper, 1954), and *The Unconscious Before Freud* (New York: Basic Books, 1960).
22. See especially Erikson's discussions of the life cycle in *Childhood and Society* and *Identity: Youth and Crisis*.
23. Erikson, *Childhood and Society*, "Conclusion: The Fear of Anxiety," pp. 359-80.
24. Susanne K. Langer, *Mind: An Essay on Human Feeling* (Baltimore: Johns Hopkins Press), Vol. I (1967) and especially Vol. II (1972), and *Philosophy in a New Key* (Cambridge, Mass.: Harvard Univ. Press, 1941); and Ernst Cassirer, *An Essay on Man* (Doubleday Anchor, 1944), *The Myth of the State* (Doubleday Anchor, 1946), and *The Philosophy of Symbolic Forms,* 3v. (New Haven: Yale Univ. Press, 1953-57).
25. Whyte, *The Next Development in Man, Accent on Form,* and *The Unconscious Before Freud.*
26. Kenneth Boulding, *The Image: Knowledge in Life and Society* (Ann Arbor: Univ. of Michigan Press, 1956).

27. See, for instance, Paul Tillich, *Systematic Theory* (Chicago: Univ. of Chicago Press, 1951), Vol. III, pp. 32-51.
28. Lifton, *Death in Life*.
29. Lifton, *Home from the War*.
30. Whyte, *The Unconscious Before Freud*, pp. 17-25.
31. Lifton, *The Broken Connection*, ms.
32. See my two essays "Protean Man" and "The Young and the Old— Notes on a New History," in *History and Human Survival*, pp. 311-73.

Chapter 4 (pages 83–112)

1. See Ernest Jones, *The Life and Work of Sigmund Freud* (New York: Basic Books, 1953), especially Vol. 1; Max Schur, *Freud: Living and Dying* (New York: International Universities Press, 1972); and also Erik H. Erikson, "The First Psychoanalyst," in *Insight and Responsibility* (New York, Norton, 1964), pp. 17-46.
2. Most of what follows can be found in Erikson, "Autobiographic Notes on the Identity Crisis," *Daedalus*, Fall 1970, pp. 730-59.
3. Jones, Vol. I, pp. 243-48.
4. Freud, "An Autobiographical Study," *Standard Edition of the Complete Psychological Works*, ed. James Strachey (London: Hogarth Press, 1953–66), Vol. XX, p. 30.
5. The approach informs all of *Childhood and Society* (New York: Norton, 1950). See also "Sex Differences in the Play Configurations of Pre-adolescents," *American Journal of Orthopsychiatry* Vol. XXI (1951), pp. 667-92; and *Observations on the Yurok: Childhood and World Image*, Univ. of California Publications in American Archaeology and Ethnology, Vol. XXXV, No. 10 (Univ. of California Press, 1943).
6. See Lifton, *History and Human Survival* (New York: Random House, 1970), introduction, pp. 3-21, and *Home from the War* (New York: Simon and Schuster, 1973), Chap. 14, "On Healing," pp. 409-42.
7. Lifton, *Thought Reform and the Psychology of Totalism: A Study of "Brainwashing" in China* (New York: Norton, 1961).
8. Lifton, *Home from the War*; see especially prologue, pp. 13-22, and Chap. 3, "Rap Groups," pp. 73-96.
9. Freud, *The Interpretation of Dreams*, in *Standard Edition*, Vol. V, pp. 351-54.
10. Erikson, "The Dream Specimen in Psychoanalysis," *Journal of the American Psychoanalytic Association*, Vol. II (1954), pp. 5-56.

11. *Ibid.*, p. 17fn.
12. Charles Fisher, informal discussion at Wellfleet, Mass., August 1973.
13. Lifton, "Youth and History" and "Images of Time," both in *History and Human Survival*, pp. 24-80.
14. Susanne K. Langer, *Mind: An Essay on Human Feeling*, Vol. II (Baltimore: Johns Hopkins Press, 1972), p. 277.
15. Langer, *op. cit.*, pp. 261-63 and 268-94, and personal communication.
16. Guntrip, "Science, Psychodynamic Reality and Autistic Thinking," p. 16.
17. Eric Olson has done most of the interviewing and is mainly responsible for the collage technique.
18. Lifton, "On Psychohistory," *Psychoanalysis and Contemporary Science*, ed. Robert R. Holt and Emanuel Peterfreund (New York: Macmillan, 1972), Vol. I, pp. 355-72; in Lifton, ed., with Olson, *Explorations in Psychohistory: The Wellfleet Papers* (New York: Simon and Schuster–Touchstone, 1974), pp. 21-41.
19. Freud, *Totem and Taboo*, in *Standard Edition*, Vol. XIII, pp. 13-161, and again in *Moses and Monotheism, Standard Edition*, Vol. XXIII, pp. 3-137.
20. William C. Bullitt and Sigmund Freud, *Thomas Woodrow Wilson, Twenty-eighth President of the United States: A Psychological Study* (Boston, Houghton Mifflin, 1967). In my paper "On Psychohistory," I state that the evidence suggests that Bullitt wrote most of the book (and Freud only the introduction) but did so from Freud's theoretical perspective.
21. See especially Philip Rieff, *Freud: The Mind of the Moralist* (New York: Viking, 1959), pp. 186-219 ("The Authority of the Past"); and "The Meaning of History and Religion in Freud's Thought," in Bruce Mazlish, ed., *Psychoanalysis in History* (Englewood Cliffs, N.J.: Prentice-Hall, 1963).
22. A further development of this perspective within Freud's struggle toward creative immortality would, I believe, help to bridge the divergent views on these disputes put forth by Jones (especially Vol. II); by Paul Roazen, *Brother Animal: The Story of Freud and Tausk* (New York: Knopf, 1969); and by Kurt Eissler, *Talent and Genius* (New York: Quadrangle Books, 1971).
23. Freud, *Civilization and Its Discontents*, in *Standard Edition*, Vol. XXI, pp. 57-145.
24. See especially Erikson, "On the Nature of Psycho-Historical Evidence: In Search of Gandhi," *Daedalus*, Summer 1968, pp. 695-

730; in Lifton, ed., with Olson, *Explorations in Psychohistory*, pp. 42-77.
25. Erikson, *Young Man Luther* (New York: Norton, 1958), pp. 151-54.
26. See especially Lifton, "On Psychohistory," *loc. cit.*; and "Images of Time" and "Protean Man," *loc. cit.*
27. Lifton, *Thought Reform*, pp. 419-72, especially 446-49.
28. Lifton, *History and Human Survival*, p. 14.
29. See Leslie H. Farber, Robert Jay Lifton, *et al.*, "Questions of Guilt," *Partisan Review*, Vol. XXXIX, No. 4 (Fall 1972), pp. 514-30; Lifton, *Home from the War*, especially Chap. 4, "Animating Guilt," and Chap. 13, "On Change"; and Martin Buber, "Guilt and Guilt Feelings," *Psychiatry*, Vol. XX, May 1957, pp. 114-29.
30. See *Home from the War*, pp. 97-133 and 388-408.
31. In a very preliminary way this model is suggested in Lifton, "The Young and the Old," in *History and Human Survival*.

Chapter 5 (pages 113–133)

1. Saul Bellow, *Herzog* (New York: Viking, 1964).
2. Lifton, *Death in Life* (New York: Random House, 1968), pp. 479-541.
3. Albert Camus, speech of acceptance upon the award of the Nobel Prize for Literature, Dec. 7, 1957.
4. All but the last quotation in this paragraph can be found in Germaine Brée, *Camus* (New Brunswick, N.J.: Rutgers Univ. Press, 1959). The last is from the Nobel Prize speech.
5. Albert Camus, *Caligula and Three Other Plays* (New York: Knopf, 1957).
6. New York: Knopf, 1946.
7. Camus, *The Rebel* (New York: Knopf, 1954).
8. New York: Knopf, 1947.
9. New York: McGraw-Hill, 1964.
10. New York: Delacorte, 1971.
11. New York: Delacorte, 1971.
12. New York: Delacorte, 1969.
13. New York: Pantheon, 1961.
14. New York: Dial Press, 1964.
15. Samuel Beckett, *Krapp's Last Tape and Other Dramatic Pieces* (New York: Grove Press, 1960).
16. Eugene Rabinowitch, "Five Years After," in Morton Grodzins and

Eugene Rabinowitch, eds., *The Atomic Age* (New York: Basic Books, 1963), p. 156.
17. New York: Knopf, 1964.

Chapter 6 (pages 135–149)

1. Richard Sennett, *The Uses of Disorder* (New York: Knopf, 1970).
2. John S. Dunne, *The Way of All the Earth* (New York: Macmillan, 1972).
3. Quotations in this paragraph are from Mircea Eliade, *Cosmos and History* (New York: Torchbooks, 1959).
4. Joseph Campbell, *The Masks of God: Primitive Mythology* (New York: Viking, 1959).
5. Francis Huxley, "Marginal Lands of the Mind," in Sir Julian Huxley, ed., *The Humanist Frame* (New York: Harper, 1961), pp. 176-77.

Chapter 7 (pages 151–171)

1. Seymour Halleck, *The Politics of Therapy* (New York: Jason Aronson, Inc., 1971).
2. See Lifton, *Home from the War* (New York: Simon and Schuster, 1973), Chap. 13, "On Change."
3. Philip Rieff, *Freud: The Mind of the Moralist* (New York: Viking, 1959), p. 27.
4. See my discussion of Freud, death, and immortality in *Home from the War*, pp. 427-32; and, more generally (concerning the great man and immortality), in *Revolutionary Immortality*.
5. Freud, letter to Martha Bernays, Nov. 15, 1883, in Ernest Jones, *The Life and Work of Sigmund Freud* (New York: Basic Books, 1953), Vol. I, pp. 175-76.
6. See especially Erikson, "Human Strength and the Cycle of Generations," in *Insight and Responsibility* (New York: Norton, 1964).
7. Lifton, "Experiments in Advocacy Research," in Jules H. Masserman, ed., *Research and Relevance*, Vol. XXI of *Science and Psychoanalysis* (New York: Grune & Stratton, 1972), pp. 259-71; and Lifton, *Home from the War*.
8. Lifton, "The Sense of Immortality: On Death and the Continuity of Life," *American Journal of Psychoanalysis*, Vol. XXXIII (1973), No. 1, pp. 3-15.
9. For detailed description of the rap-group experience, see Lifton, *Home from the War*, Chap. 3, "Rap Groups."

10. *Ibid.*, Chap. 4, "Animating Guilt."
11. *Ibid.*, Chap. 2, "America's New Survivors: The Image of My Lai."
12. For brief discussions of these issues of investigative involvement, see my introduction to *History and Human Survival* and *Thought Reform and the Psychology of Totalism*, as well as my essay "On Psychohistory."
13. Quotations and etymological sequences are from *The Oxford English Dictionary*, Vol. II, p. 2316, and *The American Heritage Dictionary*. See Lifton, *Home from the War*, Chap. 14, "On Healing."
14. Albert Camus, *Neither Victims nor Executioners* (Chicago: World Without War Publications, 1972; originally published in 1946).
15. H. Spencer Bloch, "Army Psychiatry in the Combat Zone—1967–1968," *American Journal of Psychiatry*, Vol. CXXVI (1969), pp. 291-92.
16. See *Home from the War*, Chap. 2, especially pp. 57-59.
17. Leslie Farber, "The Therapeutic Despair," in *The Ways of the Will* (New York: Basic Books, 1966).
18. Stanley Milgram, "Behavioral Study of Obedience," *Journal of Abnormal and Social Psychology*, Vol. LXVII (1963), pp. 371-78; "The Compulsion to Do Evil," *Patterns of Prejudice*, Vol. I, November–December 1967, London; and *Obedience to Authority* (New York: Harper and Row, 1974).
19. Joseph Campbell, *The Hero with a Thousand Faces* (New York: Meridian, 1956).

ABOUT THE AUTHOR

Robert Jay Lifton holds the Foundations' Fund for Research in Psychiatry professorship at Yale University.

His books include *Home from the War* (nominated for the National Book Award); *Death in Life: Survivors of Hiroshima* (which received the National Book Award in the Sciences, and the Van Wyck Brooks Award for nonfiction in 1969); *History and Human Survival; Revolutionary Immortality: Mao Tse-tung and the Chinese Cultural Revolution; Boundaries: Psychological Man in Revolution; Thought Reform and the Psychology of Totalism: A Study of "Brainwashing" in China; Crimes of War* (with Richard A. Falk and Gabriel Kolko); *Living and Dying* (with Eric Olson); and *Explorations in Psychohistory: The Wellfleet Papers* (edited with Eric Olson).

He is married to Betty Jean Lifton, the writer, and they have two children.

Index

183